MW01167038

what people are saying about
Testimony of a Kept Woman

"A soul opened to God's healing will be restored. *Testimony of a Kept Woman* is a dynamic testament of God's restoring grace. As you open this book, you immediately begin the journey through twenty-two years of emotional, mental, physical and spiritual abuse. Thank God, it does not end there! You will read about a wife's suffering, feel her pain, share her joy, witness her victory—and finally—you will find encouragement. This is no ordinary story. It is yesterday's darkness, life unfolding, and God reshaping and adorning His precious vessel of honor."

—Brook Lynn Dorcent
author of *Missing the Mark*

"*Testimony of a Kept Woman* is a disturbing yet enlightening book about the real life experiences of one Christian woman of courage who was first married to a bipolar man and later to a sociopath. Both marriages end tragically, but her life moves forward victoriously. A good read."

—Dr. Howard W. Parker Jr.
pastor of Sycamore Hill Missionary Baptist Church
president of General Baptist State
Convention of North Carolina, Inc.

"*Testimony of a Kept Woman* is an awesome book that testifies of how God delivered, healed, and set free a woman with purpose who was married to a man with bipolar disorder and later to a sociopath. Both husbands tried to ensnare her with intimidation, domestic violence, spiritual and emotional abuse… but her Third Husband (God Almighty) proclaimed liberty and has chosen her for greatness, has given her beauty for ashes and a garment of praise for the spirit of heaviness, and has put her on display for His splendor."

—Minister Lola Thompson
founder and president of Women with Purpose

"Janice Newell-Byrd's story of resilience and perseverance is a testimony of her faith. Her personal triumph through abuse and rejection has made her the phenomenal woman she is today. Women of every faith, race and denomination can relate to this story. If they've never heard or seen a woman of the church suffer for what she believed in, then they need to read this book. Her story is like no other."

—Lynnette Taylor
anchor and reporter for WITN- TV News Anchor
Greenville, NC

"*Testimony of a Kept Woman* provides the reader with an insider's view of living with domestic violence and emotional abuse while trying to live a 'normal' life. Jan's story is a journey from pain to redemption that leaps off the pages in its telling. It's a must read."

—Mark S. Woodson
president of 1570AM–WECU
Gospel Radio, Greenville, NC
author of *I Couldn't Ride With My Father*

"Jan Newell-Byrd's book, *Testimony of a Kept Woman*, parallels so many untold stories of spousal abuse: mental, physical and emotional. Her story is not only one of survival, but she has been blessed to triumph in spite of what she has endured. Her journey of endurance, survival and triumph is rooted in her steadfast faith in God. Now that she has shared her story, prayerfully it will be an encouragement to others who may have struggled through or perhaps are still struggling with these or similar challenges in life. Remember: never give up on God, because He never gives up on you, regardless of how bad things may seem at the time."

—Dante D. Wright I
senior pastor of Sweet Home
Baptist Church of Round Rock
Round Rock, TX

"Testimony of a Kept Woman is a contemporary compilation of experiential spiritually transforming vignettes and scriptural tried and trues which compel introspection through reflections into the life journey of one sold out to her God. Read, weep, learn, and grow in Christ!

—Reverend Sidney A. Locks, Jr.
pastor of Cornerstone Missionary Baptist Church
Greenville, NC

testimony
of a kept
woman

testimony

of a kept

woman

From Misery to Ministry
Instead of the State Penitentiary
Jan Newell-Byrd

TATE PUBLISHING
AND ENTERPRISES, LLC

Published by Tate Publishing & Enterprises, LLC
127 E. Trade Center Terrace | Mustang, Oklahoma 73064 USA
1.888.361.9473 | www.tatepublishing.com

Tate Publishing is committed to excellence in the publishing industry. The company reflects the philosophy established by the founders, based on Psalm 68:11,
"The Lord gave the word and great was the company of those who published it."

Book design copyright © 2012 by Tate Publishing, LLC. All rights reserved.
Cover design by Leah LeFlore
Interior design by Stephanie Woloszyn

Published in the United States of America

ISBN: 978-1-61862-943-2
1. Religion / Christian Life / Inspirational
2. Biography & Autobiography / Personal Memoirs
12.05.23

dedication

This book is dedicated to my Lord and Savior Jesus Christ, for His love, grace, mercy, and shield of protection during the many years I lived as a victim of domestic violence and emotional abuse. He knows how reluctant and resistant I was to His idea of writing and exposing my experiences for others to read and judge. However, I now want to thank the Lord for constantly reminding me that it was never about me; it's all about Him. And over a period of ten long, tedious years, His sovereign will has prevailed, and at long last this book has been birthed into existence. May the Lord Jesus Christ receive glory, honor, and the highest praise for all He has done for me and the many others like me. I will bless the Lord at all times…for this book is *all about JESUS.*

acknowledgments

To my wonderful parents, John Wesley Townsend and Janie Temple Townsend, who raised me to be a loving, caring, and independent woman of God.

To my adult children, S. Wesley Newell, Mark Anthony Newell, Ronda Janis Byrd, and daughter-in-law, Dana Benton Newell, for their unconditional love, loyalty, and encouragement.

To my three amazing grandchildren, Morgan, Melani, and Jeremiah, for their unending love and devotion.

To my sister, Ada Bass, for her tremendous insight and godly wisdom.

To my three close childhood friends, Lady Em Williams, Joan Geraldine Wright, and Virginia Pierce Toms, who helped shape my personality during those formative years.

To my close adult friends and confidants, Paulette Smallwood, Michele Pearson, and Jenifra Madison, for their strong faith and commitment to Jesus Christ and their confidence in me.

To Jean Blount, for her sensitivity, expertise, and willingness to help me cross my t's and dot my i's.

To both of my former husbands, for without either one, I would never have become the woman of God I am today.

To those who offered book endorsements, including Rev. Dr. Howard W. Parker Jr., president of the

General Baptist State Convention of North Carolina Inc. and pastor of Sycamore Hill Missionary Baptist Church of Greenville, NC; Rev. Sidney A. Locks Jr., pastor of Cornerstone Missionary Baptist Church of Greenville, NC; Rev. Dr. Dante Wright I, lead pastor of Sweet Home Baptist Church of Round Rock, TX; author Brook Lynn Dorcent; author Mark Woodson Sr.; Min. Lola Thompson; Lynnette Taylor, WITN News TV Anchor; and special thanks to Rev. Gaylon C. Clark, lead pastor of the Greater Mount Zion Baptist Church of Austin, TX, for writing the forward to this book.

To the Tate Publishing Staff for believing in my book when so many other publishers refused to invest in a novice.

To the males and females all over the world who have ever suffered under the subtle or strong arm tactics of a physical or psychological abuser. May God's love, grace, and mercy liberate you to never again fear anyone except our Lord and Savior Jesus Christ.

If I have overlooked anyone in offering thanks and acknowledgments, I ask them to charge it to my head and not my heart.

table of contents

PART FOUR 213
Healing and Renewal

foreword

Though at times it doesn't always seem like it, God's timing is great! Let me explain.

In June 2000, Jan Newell-Byrd had a conversation with her pastor-husband in Round Rock, Texas, that would mark the beginning of the end of their twenty-two year marriage. That same month, my wife and son, Kathy and Michael, joined me in Austin, Texas, for what was the beginning of our new beginning—the beginning of the best chapters in our family. I started as a pastor at the Greater Mount Zion Baptist Church, twenty miles south of Round Rock in May, but my family relocated to join me the following month.

In September, 2000, Jan had a vision that her husband was trying to destroy her. I had a vision that God was trying to use me as I was officially installed as Greater Mount Zion's pastor.

In March, 2001, Jan was served divorce papers by husband number two. I was celebrating the one-year anniversary of my trial sermon at the church that had become family. Two people! Two dissimilar realities! Yet God had set a time for our histories to collide.

In October, 2001, I preached a revival in Round Rock, Texas, for her former husband. God apparently used me to minister to her daughter who urged Jan to attend the revival. She sat in the back of the church where she had experienced so much pain and heard me preach on *Love as a Lifestyle* from 1 Corinthians 13. Though I didn't know it, God was doing something in Jan's heart that Thursday evening that would make both of our lives better.

In December, 2001, she joined our church. I didn't know who she was until others informed me. "She's a former pastor's wife who was recently divorced. I think she's going through a lot right now," a member shared. I heard God whispering to me, "Let her heal. Let me do what I need to do in her life." I didn't want to be overly aggressive in offering support. I wanted God to have his way.

We soon developed a relationship. Jan began sending me e-mails of appreciation for my Sunday sermons. Hers was not a random, general gratitude. She didn't say things like "Good job, Pastor!" or "Really enjoyed your message." She took copious notes and shared specific ways the message inspired her to think, feel, and act more like Jesus. Quickly, I realized I was dealing with an exceptional soul. Jan had a ravenous hunger for God. But there was more. She was trying to encourage me! She wanted me to feel what she felt and know what I was doing mattered to her and others. Like clockwork, I would read my e-mail from Jan on Monday morning. I affectionately began calling her "my encourager!" As a young pastor still finding his voice and leadership identity, her words added more courage to my natural passion.

I discovered that Jan had exceptional abilities to teach. We started a women's ministry, and Jan was one of the primary teachers. Her lessons were life-giving. I even started asking her to teach on Sundays, occasionally. She was initially uncomfortable because she had been taught women should not preach. I assured her she did not have to define what she was doing as preaching. She was just talking for God and using her teaching gift—like she did in other venues. Her gifts grew and blossomed! Our women loved her, and our men respected her gift to teach. Jan was one of the most influential leaders in our church at that time. When she moved to North Carolina in 2006, I cried! Real tears!

Yet I had no idea how many tears *she* had cried! It's 5:30 a.m. on December 30, 2010. I just finished reading the book you are holding in your hands. I'd heard rumors of infidelities in her marriage but did not pry. I wanted to be safe for Jan. I didn't want her to ever think I was concerned about her past. Much of what is in this book is something I am just now learning! I didn't know she had survived two traumatic divorces and bounced back from physical and emotional abuse. She came out of a marriage of dysfunction followed by another marriage of deception with deeper affection for the one she married first—Jesus. She has no discernible scars! She is the most profoundly Christian woman I know!

Jan's story is one of grace! There's grace for every place in life. God squeezes purpose out of every pain. This book should be required reading for everyone who desires to get married or has had their dignity challenged by an abuser. Jan Newell-Byrd has come through the fire, but she doesn't smell like smoke! Let Jan's story encourage you, upset you, humor you, depress you, and, ultimately, strengthen you. Because she's endured the flames, you don't have to!

—Gaylon Clark, Lead Pastor of the Greater
Mount Zion Baptist Church of Austin, TX

introduction

The Classic Crime Scene

The date is Monday, September 25, 2000. I am returning home, having just facilitated one of the best Sunday school teachers' meetings I have been to in a long time. As a wife, mother, Christian Education Director, Sunday school teacher, and First Lady of the church all rolled into one, I finally feel that I am beginning to understand and master the challenges I face within my various roles in the ministry. I believe that God's work is beginning to manifest itself.

I walk alone from the church back to my home in the serene community where I live. I am acutely aware of my tranquil surroundings. It is a crisp, autumn evening, and the night sky is filled with millions of twinkling stars. The full moon is shining brightly, and I can see the perfectly manicured lawns of my neighbors as I pass their houses. I am energetic, upbeat, and jubilant. Life is good, and I am happy to be alive.

My Mind Drifts to My Marriage...

...I hear the sound of footsteps behind me. They pick up speed as they approach. Terrified, I turn to see a man hurling down the once quiet street headed straight toward me. He is imposing and dressed in black from head to toe with a hood covering his face. He is also holding what appears to be a revolver in his hand. Before I can scream for help, he is upon me, and I am paralyzed with fright! I can't move! Just as he closes in on me to pull the trigger, I manage to snatch the hood back from his face. To my shock and horror, I recognize the mugger! In sheer astonishment, I realize that this assailant who is about to take my life is none other than my own pastor... my husband. Before I can plead with him to spare me, the gun fires at point blank range. I feel the horrific impact of hot, angry metal as it rips and punctures my body, my soul, and my spirit. I double over in blinding pain and crumple to the ground. As I lie there with my face pressed into the cool, damp grass, I am able to see the intruder out of one eye as he stands over me, glaring down in disgust. Silently, he turns, flees down the street, and disappears into the menacing shadows of the night.

I am utterly stunned... I am bewildered, bleeding, confused, screaming hysterically, and crying out in pain and disbelief. My mind races with a frantic jumble of questions. *What just happened? Was that really my husband that shot me? No, it couldn't be... but I know without a doubt that it was! But why would the man I loved and married want to shoot me? What did I ever do to provoke such an evil outburst? Is there some mistake?*

My Mind Returns to the Present...

The placid fall evening is as undisturbed as it was when I first began to daydream. There was no gunman... no bullet... no blood. But still, my husband had meant to destroy me. The setting may have been his study... and the bullets may have been his words. But my emotions are real. It is exactly how I felt when I heard my husband and pastor of almost twenty-two years coldly say to me, "Our marriage is over. I don't love you any more, and I am divorcing you!" The feelings are as real as those in this reoccurring nightmare to which I so often return.

What do you do when your whole world has blown apart?

What do you do when the tears won't stop flowing and you moan and groan in the agony of indescribable pain—pain that seemingly has no remedy or relief? Well, if you are a woman of God, you do what you have been biblically taught to do—pray! Right? Right! You go boldly and fervently to the throne of grace, and you pour out your heart to God.

But what do you do if heaven is silent, and even God Almighty appears to have packed up, moved away, and forgotten to leave you His forwarding address? What do you do then?

Do you give up, falling into despair and self-destructive behavior?

Absolutely not! You remember that God is sovereign and that there are no accidents in the journey called life. You remember that God has a plan and a purpose for your life and that no devil in Hell can deny you your God-given destiny if you stand on the foundation of faith and hope. Like David, you encourage yourself (1 Samuel 30:6). For all who put their hope in the Lord will be strong and brave (Psalm 31:24). Like Joseph, you remember God can turn into good what others meant for evil (Genesis 50:20). It matters not what happens to you as much as how you respond to what has happened to you. From this experience, one can either become bitter and retreat into a shell or become better and use this horrific experience and move from misery to ministry. The latter is what I have chosen.

Hopefully you will be able to identify and sympathize with someone who has struggled and failed repeatedly and yet experienced victory in the end through Jesus Christ. If you do not judge me too harshly, I think you might enjoy reading this recollection of my journey— *Testimony of a Kept Woman: From Misery to Ministry Instead of the State Penitentiary.*

Read! Reflect! Enjoy!

—Jan Newell-Byrd

As the Lord was with Joseph
(Genesis 37-50),
so the Lord has been with Jan...

PART ONE

the anatomy of a physically abusive relationship

Vincent was always irritable, angry, or upset about one thing or another. His fluctuating moods were as erratic and unpredictable as the weather in the Midwest where we lived. In the olden days, people who "acted differently" were not labeled bipolar or diagnosed with OCD (obsessive compulsive disorder), nor medicated, as they are today. They were just considered peculiar, and Vincent was peculiar, indeed. Even so, I cared deeply for him and didn't understand why he constantly directed his negative behavior toward me. When anything went wrong for him, he would always say it was my fault. Why would he take out his frustrations on me when I was about the only person that would put up with him and his weird ways? His actions were hurtful and made me want to pull away from him.

However, one unusually quiet and pleasant evening, Vincent and I were enjoying some rare shared time together at home. It was marvelous. We were laughing, playing around, and having a great time together at the kitchen table in our small apartment. It wasn't long, though, before Vincent's mood changed, and he became volatile for no apparent reason. He began to nit-pick at me, waiting for me to respond with anything that would make him feel justified for being angry with me. Now, I had learned long ago that trying to reason with him during times like this was futile. Vincent would purposely misconstrue anything I said and then turn it against me. So this time I didn't say a word. I simply held my tongue, although it was hard to do. I knew keeping my mouth shut and my thoughts to myself would generally be the best way to handle this kind of domestic crisis.

But this time was different. Even though I never said a word, my silence only seemed to infuriate Vincent that much more. Then slowly, without warning, he rose from his chair, came over to the other side of the table where I was sitting, and began shoving me. When that did not prompt a response, he then began hitting me. Finally, I had had enough of his abuse. I might have been skinny, but I was as strong as an ox. I stood up, balled my fist, took perfect aim, and socked Vincent smack dab in the middle of his mouth as hard as I could. The blow was so powerful that it knocked him backward and onto the floor. It was one of the sweetest and most satisfying emotions I had ever experienced. However, I knew that by the time Vincent finally picked himself up from the floor, there would be hell to pay. So, I did what any sane person would do…I ran for my life!

Faster than lightning, I dashed out the kitchen from our small, one-bedroom apartment, down a flight of stairs, out the front door, up the street, and around the corner. I was running as fast as my skinny legs would carry me. When Vincent and I married in 1959, I weighed only ninety-five pounds. After being married to him for less than a year, I had lost nearly ten. I must have looked like a pitiful sight, but I was still feisty, and I could run like the wind. Naturally, Vincent gave chase. He was immediately on my heels, but eventually I was able to pull away. While running, I thought to myself, *Now, what do I do? Where can I go?* I didn't even have enough money to catch the trolley to my parents' home, as I had left my purse in the apartment in my haste to flee Vincent. Nor did I have any real friends close by to turn to for help. Even though I was gregarious and loved meeting people, I hadn't taken the time to get to know any of my neighbors since Vincent didn't want us to socialize with anyone. Although I didn't realize it at the time, his goal had been to keep me isolated so that I wouldn't talk to other people and learn that our marriage and way of life were not normal. My mind was racing as fast as my legs were carrying me, and I began to reflect back on my life and ponder some thought provoking questions: *What was going to happen to me? And how in the world did I get myself into this precarious predicament?*

Off to College and
How I Met Husband Number One

In the twenty-fifth chapter of 1 Samuel, there is an intriguing story about a married couple named Nabal and Abigail. Verse three says, "She was a wise and beautiful woman, but her husband was a fool!" (1 Samuel 25:2-3).

A logical question is, "How did these two opposites get together?" Also, "Why did Abigail marry Nabal?" The biblical account is an interesting story filled with enigmatic twists and turns about a couple who seemed quite different. It is true that opposites attract and marry. I know because it happened to me. It all started one Friday in October 1958 when I didn't have a ride home from college.

Starting College

After graduating from West Philadelphia High School in June 1957, I switched my major from music to elementary education. That decision caused a financial hardship because we could no longer depend on my music scholarship to pay my way through college. However, my parents knew I would be happier teaching in a classroom rather than traveling around the country with male musicians in an orchestra or band. I spent that summer applying to various teacher colleges. When I received my acceptance letter from Cheyney State, my parents and I were overjoyed—especially my dad. Having his daughter attend college was a life-long dream come true.

Cheyney State Teachers College (now Cheyney State University) is the oldest historically Black college or university in the United States. Cheyney was a small four-year teaching college built by the Quakers in the mid-nineteenth century. It is an excellent school that has produced outstanding teachers. My first day on campus was both thrilling and traumatic. I was nervous and excited at the same time. The first person I met was Florence E. Long. I could tell by her wide-eyed expression that she was scared to death, and so was I. Neither of us had any idea of what to expect as college students. Immediately, we struck up a friendship that has lasted throughout the years. Flo (as I call her) lived on campus, but due to a lack of funds, I continued to live at home. I commuted back and forth every day just as I had done in high school.

Living in a large metropolitan city like Philadelphia would pose no transportation problem. One could easily get wherever one needed to go by simply hopping on a bus, trolley, subway, or El Train. However, Cheyney University was not in Philly. The college was located about twenty-five miles outside the city limits, and back in the fifties, no public transportation to the school was provided. Only one train ran there twice a week at odd times. To make matters worse, Cheyney had been placed in the beautiful woods of Pennsylvania away from the main highway. Therefore, commuting students needed a car to get back and forth on those winding back roads.

My problem was simple. I needed transportation to commute to college each day, but I didn't have a car. Even though I worked, I never managed to save enough to purchase even a small, used car or an old, reliable truck. My transportation worries were resolved, however, when I met a group of upper classmates who were sensitive to my situation and decided to adopt me as their younger sister. Johnnie, one of the group members, had a brand new car that her parents had purchased for her. She was willing to let me commute with her along with two other riders. Each of us paid Johnnie five dollars a day (or twenty-five dollars a week), which included door-to-door round trip service to and from school. Our fares helped pay for her gas and earned her extra spending money. It was a win-win situation for all concerned.

Later when I told Flo about my good fortune, she informed me that "my big sisters" were all members of Delta Sigma Theta, Inc., the sorority that we both wanted to pledge. What a blessing! A year later, both Flo and I pledged Delta.

My first year of college life at Cheyney State University was great. I was gaining a tremendous education, meeting lots of friends, and having the time of my life, but that was all about to change.

Needing Transportation

Johnnie was a good and dependable driver who seldom missed a day of picking us up. However, on those rare occasions when she did not drive, I was left high and dry to find other transportation. On one particular Friday in October, 1958, Johnnie did not drive home. She decided to stay over for the football game and dance; therefore, I had to find another ride home. I wasn't upset. I just headed for the parking lot to look for a ride with someone else. The only student around was Vincent.

Vincent was a sophomore, and although he and I had some classes together, I doubt seriously if we had ever exchanged two words. He was not the average second-year college student. He was twenty-three years old, and like most of the other students in our class, I was only eighteen and still a teenager. We were all very young, but compared to us, Vincent was old.

Vincent wasn't just a full grown man; he was worldly. He had served four years in the Korean War, traveled abroad, and was now attending college on the G.I. Bill. While most of us sophomores were going to college to obtain a degree in education, to socialize, to get away from home, and to find that significant other, Vincent was there to get an education. His goal was to learn all he could in order to prepare himself to graduate, obtain a teaching position, and make an adequate living for himself. He was intelligent, mature, focused, and serious about his studies. He was an honor student. All these were positive traits that made us look up to Vincent with admiration, even though he didn't know it.

Vincent also had a bit of a reputation. He was referred to as "different." I had heard students mention Vincent's name in somewhat vague and uncomplimentary terms. However, I was not one to listen to gossip or innuendo about another person. Perhaps this particular time, I should have paid attention. I might have learned some valuable information.

Vincent was a loner, and while that didn't classify him as being different in and of itself, he rarely socialized. He went to class alone, he ate alone, and when he was not in class, he spent most of his time in the library, studying… alone. He didn't seem to like people very much. Since it appeared he wanted to be left alone, people, for the most part, left him alone. At times, Vincent seemed agitated, irritable, or upset about something, but then he'd appear all right. His moods were rather unpredictable.

If there was one crucial thing that made Vincent stand out as different, like an eye sore, it was his car. Vincent was an absolute fanatic when it came to his car, and that is no exaggeration. The rumor around campus was that Vincent never wanted anyone to park too close to him out of fear that his car's paint might get chipped. So in order to avoid this from happening, Vincent would straddle two parking spaces. Now that might not have been a problem if there had been adequate parking spaces for all the students, but that was not the case. Finding a place to park in the morning was always difficult, even for the "early birds." But for late comers, it was almost impossible to find a space and get to first period class on time. Late students coming in from Philly would seemingly fly down those dangerous, winding back roads at break-neck speed. Screeching tires could be heard from any point on campus at the same time every morning. The scene was more like an airport landing field than a college parking lot. Then those same students would scramble to find a spot to park, hop out of their cars, and run like crazy to make it to class before the first bell rang. Not surprisingly, it was the same students every morning—but not Vincent. The military had taught him discipline and timeliness. As a matter of fact, Vincent was on the campus so early that he could easily find two parking spaces and use both of them.

Pretty soon, however, word got out about what Vincent was doing. A few students who were not easily intimidated decided they needed to teach him a lesson in courtesy. They began to scheme how they could get back at him and agitate him, just for the fun of it. Periodically, one or two students would purposely park their cars as close to Vincent's car as they could. Then they would watch to see his reaction when he came to the parking lot. As predicted, Vincent would be furious and explode in anger. His outbursts were horrible. Eventually, he got the reputation for being "different."

All this time, however, I was completely oblivious to what was going on. Don't ask me why I didn't know. Perhaps it was because I was not driving and didn't have to park. I really don't know. What I *do* know is that my main concern each morning was how quickly I could hop out of Johnnie's car, run, and get to class myself. You see, I was always one of those late ones. Consequently, I missed all the drama in the college parking lot. However, I did eventually learn (a little too late) about it.

Stranded and Rescued

That Friday, I stood in the parking lot, thinking I might be stranded. At first, I didn't see any other students. It seemed that everyone had stayed over for the game and dance. As I think back, it was rather strange that I hadn't stayed that particular evening because I usually went to most school events. But for one reason or another, I decided to go home. I looked over the parking lot again, and this time I saw someone. It was Vincent. He, too, was not staying for the dance and was heading back to Philly. I didn't know it then, but Vincent never stayed over for any games or parties. He always went straight home.

When I saw Vincent walking toward his car, I was so relieved at not being stranded that I called out to him. He had also seen me standing in the parking lot and said, "Hi! Do you need a ride home?"

Although I was a little hesitant about riding with Vincent that evening, I said, "Yes, I surely do. Thank you." I hopped into his car.

That fateful Friday, October, 1958, changed my life forever.

Two Wrongs Don't Make a Right

After that fateful ride, Vincent and I began dating. I was popular and had lots of platonic boyfriends my age on campus, but pretty soon Vincent and I dated exclusively. My mom and dad were not particularly pleased with our growing relationship. They both felt that Vincent was too old and much too mature for me socially, and rightfully so. I had been sheltered as a youngster, and they would have been more comfortable had I continued to date young men closer to my age. They decided to accept our relationship, however, because I had never caused them problems, plus they knew they had raised me well. Still, I sensed their growing concerns but decided to dismiss them. The rational part of me wanted them to sit me down and give me an ultimatum, but they never did. The fact that they didn't was strange, because we were a close knit family who talked about everything.

As I look back, I wish they had openly expressed their doubts, fears, and misgivings about Vincent. Maybe my life would have been different, but then again, maybe not. You see, I had a "hard head," my parents' term for being headstrong. I guess this was one of those times that they allowed me to choose my own path, knowing that if it were the wrong one, I would learn a lesson I would take with me to my grave. And what a lesson I learned!

Shortly after we began dating, I lost my virginity in the back seat of Vincent's 1953 Chevy, parked in Fairmount Park in Philly. It wasn't romantic. It wasn't gentle. It wasn't even good. For Vincent, I do believe it was just "something to do." He was "experienced." I wasn't, and it was the worst thing that could have ever happened to me. I was completely devastated, humiliated, bleeding, and traumatized. Having sex before marriage was terrible enough! But to "do it" for the very first time in the back seat of a car!...in the dark!...and in the city park! Oh, my God! What was I thinking? How could I have done this...and in this way? This had to be the unpardonable sin. I was sure it was, and I knew I was going straight to hell. I was grief stricken.

The shame and the guilt would plague me for years to come. I felt filthy, common, soiled and defiled. I knew I was a *sinner*. And I knew lots about sin, because I had heard numerous "fire and brimstone" sermons at Holy Temple Church of God in Christ while growing up. I had sung many hymns about sin, but there was one hymn in particular that had made a real impression on me. The lyrics said, "*Yield not to temptation, for yielding is sin!* Yes, I had yielded or given in to Vincent, and now I stood wondering how I could have been such an idiot. Oh, but what I hadn't heard preached was the grace and mercy of an all-wise, all-loving, and all-merciful God. What I hadn't heard was that Christ had died for me on the cross and redeemed me from the curse of the law (Galatians 3:13). What I didn't know was that I had been forgiven for my past, present, and future sins by the blood of Jesus according to the riches of His grace (Ephesians 1:7). And, oh, what I hadn't heard and didn't know would hurt me. What I didn't know and hadn't heard would put me in bondage for years and years to come. And because I didn't know the whole truth of God, I felt that I was the biggest sinner in the whole wide world. Whoever said ignorance is bliss lied. So in order to redeem myself and rectify my sinful soul, in my way of thinking, there was only one thing left for me to do... *get married*! So at the tender age of nineteen while still a sophomore in college, I accepted Vincent's proposal of marriage.

And the Lord was with Jan...

engagement number one: the handwriting on the wall

In the same hour came forth fingers of a man's hand, and wrote against the candlestick upon the plaster of the wall of the king's palace: and the king saw the part of the hand that wrote.

Daniel 5:5 (KJV)

If you are a child of God, He will send you warnings of impending danger in various ways. God will never leave His children unaware. Our Heavenly Father loves His spiritual children and desires to protect them from danger, much like the way that loving earthly parents want to do for their offspring. God always gives us a "heads-up" before we get into trouble.

My Problem was that I Never Listened.

During my engagement to Vincent in our third year of college, many friends and family members tried to point out some of the obvious warning signs regarding Vincent. I listened to them politely, but I had already made up my mind. God Himself even gave me two clear warnings that should have given me pause before jumping into marriage.

One sign was Vincent's violent temper. During most of our courtship, Vincent kept his emotions under control. He was quite skillful in doing so. He would socialize with my family and friends, but the time spent with them would be short. His conversations would be minimal, and when they *did* occur, they were focused on sports or trivial subject matter. Nothing of substance was ever discussed. Vincent was able to mask his true feelings about situations by either smiling, keeping silent, or evading the issue by walking away. He never addressed controversial or confrontational subjects. Any woman with an ounce of sense should have been able to read the handwriting on the wall. I was either as blind as a bat, stupid, or just in love.

Warning Signs

One evening during our engagement, Vincent and I took a drive out to Fairmont Park, which was a recreational area with beautiful gardens, winding roads, and hiking trails near the middle of the city. We parked overlooking a scenic area and were discussing plans for our upcoming wedding. Suddenly, Vincent became agitated. To this day, I do not know exactly what I said to trigger his hostile and aggressive reaction, but I definitely remember how upset he was. He jumped out of the car, slammed his door shut, and stormed around to the passenger's side of the car where I was sitting. He opened the door and began yelling at me.

I was so shocked by this violent outburst that I couldn't even respond to him. My passive behavior only angered him even further. He drove his fist into the small vent window at the front of the passenger window. As the glass shattered, his hand began to bleed profusely. Instinctively, I grabbed his hand to try to help him, but he angrily pulled away from me. Pulling a handkerchief from his pocket, he wrapped it around his hand, got back into the car, and drove me home.

We never spoke of that unpleasant incident in the park again. We both pretended that it had never happened.

Disturbing Premonitions

The other incident was even clearer. Two weeks before the wedding, the Lord gave me another premonition about my impending marriage. I had a disturbing vision of my life married to Vincent.

In it, I was walking in a sunny field where trees were flourishing and flowers were blooming. The atmosphere was very peaceful. As I looked across this lovely field, I could see threatening storm clouds rolling across toward me. In those ominous clouds, I could see the hail and torrential rains that were converging upon me. The wind was uprooting trees and shredding flowers, whipping them violently in all directions. The tranquility had vanished and was replaced by chaos and terror. My heart raced as I was swept up by the wind and cast into the maelstrom of noise and turbulence. This vision of mine was so frightening that I was paralyzed and bewildered for several minutes afterward.

If that were not a warning from the Lord about my future with Vincent, I don't know what it could have been. I was shaken to my very core. I no longer felt confident about marriage. True, I loved him, but I felt very uneasy and realized that I should not go through with this wedding.

I had been standing at the top of the stairs in my parents' home when I had the vision, and my immediate response was to tell them that I was sorry for disrupting all of our plans but that I simply could not marry a man about whom I was beginning to feel so uncertain. But they had spent so much money on this wedding—money that they could ill afford, money they had saved and borrowed to ensure that their oldest daughter could have a memorable wedding that she would treasure forever.

As I started down the steps to break the news to Mom and Dad, the doorbell rang. My mom answered the door while Dad continued building the temporary shelf that would display all the wedding gifts that had already begun pouring in. I remember Mom warmly greeting one of their old friends, Mrs. Covington. She smiled and congratulated my parents for successfully raising such a "mature and intelligent Christian daughter." I remember thinking to myself, *Intelligent? Me? Yeah, right!* Mrs. Covington continued with the accolades as both of my parents beamed with pride.

I quietly tried to duck out of sight. I could give my parents the news about my decision not to go through with the wedding after Mrs. Covington had left. Unfortunately, Mrs. Covington spotted me at the top of the stairs and asked to hug the future bride. As I turned, I could see a large, beautifully wrapped wedding gift in her hands. She insisted that I open her gift immediately so that it, too, could be displayed. Reluctantly, I turned, descended the stairs, and gave her a hug and a kiss. At her insistence, I opened her gift. Inside was a four-piece, silver canister set. It was beautiful and very expensive— just what I had wanted for my kitchen but had never imagined that I would actually have. Back then, couples waited and saved to get what they needed or wanted, or they put the item on lay-away, paying small amounts until the balance could be paid in full.

Standing there in the hallway, without praying and without consulting the good judgment of loved ones wiser than I, I made a decision that affected not only my life but the lives of my children as well—years before they were born.

I decided to continue with my wedding rather than bring shame to my parents by calling it off. In retrospect, someone might have asked, "Didn't you know that this man was not normal?"

"Yes and no," would be my reply.

Vincent and I met and married in the late fifties when society did not diagnose and label mental ill-

nesses. Even so, I wish that I had talked with someone older and wiser about Vincent's violent temper and
fickle personality. Never would I tell anyone to ignore
the behavior that I was experiencing.

I took my destiny into my own hands. It never
dawned on me then that a failed and broken marriage (with children who would have to suffer the
consequences with me) was far worse than the possible shame of calling off my wedding. I should *never*
have made a decision without consulting God about
the matter. The Lord gave me warning after warning,
telling me, "Don't rush into marriage. Take your time,
and be absolutely sure you should marry him." I simply
chose not to heed the voice of God.

Why didn't I listen? I felt that I knew more about
Vincent than God. That may sound ridiculous (it certainly does to me now), but I thought that I could
change Vincent once we were married. I saw something in him that no one else saw, and I felt that he
needed me. How naïve I was!

I now know better. Only the work of the Holy Spirit
can transform a person by renewing the mind. But not
even the Holy Spirit could have given common sense
to a young woman determined to go through life with
her eyes shut tightly, refusing to submit to his teaching.

Angels Fear to Tread, but Fools Rush Right In

Soon after that decision to go through with the wedding, I went from gregarious to melancholy. People
noticed the change, but they attributed it to exhaustion

from working so hard on wedding preparations and college assignments. After my premonition, I felt as if I had slipped from the warmth of the sun into chilling darkness. The depth of this darkness was overwhelming because of the guilt that I carried for not having consulted with God or my parents about the biggest decision of my life. I was trapped. I felt as if I would have to stay in this marriage since I had made the decision. After all, I was getting what I deserved.

My grandmother had a saying, "If you make your bed hard, you will have to lie in it." I made my own bed very hard with that ill-fated decision, and I lay in it for nearly twenty years—to my regret and that of my two sons. God takes care of babies, drunks, and fools, and while I was neither a baby nor drunk, I certainly qualified as a fool!

God has been good to me through all of my illogical thinking and through all of my mistakes and misjudgments. His hand has been on my life every step of the way. God has never left or forsaken me, and He is still working his plan for me in His own way and His own time. Those dark years spent in a turbulent marriage taught me to lean on Him in times of strife and to depend on His blessings. With patience and persistence, Jesus taught me how to transform my troubles into His triumphs.

My God was faithful, even when I was not.

And the Lord was with Jan...

my un-blissful wedding day and beyond: a roller coaster marriage

We are troubled on every side, yet not distressed; we are perplexed, but not in despair; persecuted, but not forsaken; cast down, but not destroyed.

2 Corinthians 12:8-9, KJV

Wrong from the Start

A woman's wedding day should be the happiest day of her life. Mine wasn't. Vincent and I were married on Thanksgiving Day in 1959, a day that was cold and overcast. God only knows how my parents found the money to pull off our splendid church wedding, which was attended by hundreds. Everything was beautiful—the church, the ceremony, the reception, the guests—everything that is, except the couple for whom all of these preparations had been made.

Highway to Hell

The splendor of my great day was completely spoiled when we got into an argument while standing in the receiving line during the reception. An old high school friend kissed me on the cheek and shook Vincent's hand to congratulate us on our marriage. After the friend had walked away, Vincent pinched me on my arm as hard as he could and hissed in my ear, "How long have you been sleeping with him?" I couldn't believe my ears, and I thought that I might faint right there in the receiving line.

Still, I wasn't about to let him get away with such an insult. I immediately pinched him back and whispered, "Never, you fool," while continuing to force a smile and greet our guests.

By the time that we climbed into the wedding car (decorated by our best man to drive the "happy couple" around the city with the horn blaring, as was the custom of that day), we were nearly at blows in the back seat. Little did I know that climbing into that car marked the beginning of my ride to hell and back, which would last almost twenty years.

Is the Honeymoon Over?

Vincent and I married during mid-term testing, so we spent our honeymoon weekend studying. We never had a normal honeymoon. Being married, going to college, and working all at the same time made life for us extremely difficult. After our marriage, Vincent's G.I. Bill increased a whopping ten dollars. Instead of $240 per month, we began receiving $250. Wow!

As a young and poor college student, I learned to make pancakes creatively by mixing discounted flour with water (syrup was made in an equally economical fashion, using sugar and water). My pancakes were a budget blessing from heaven. Once we ate two or three, we didn't need to eat again until the next day. We didn't eat the finest of food or the healthiest of meals, but by God's grace and mercy we survived. Neither Vincent nor I ever missed a day of class on account of sickness while we were in college, either. God was so good to us.

We had all of our classes together, and this arrangement improved my grades immensely. Vincent was a brilliant student with a nearly perfect grade point average, and he taught me how to study. I even began to enjoy researching and spending time in the library, which was something that I had loathed before we were married.

We got along well while we were in school study-ing, but the moment we came home in the evenings, the bickering would begin. During our marriage, I had never heard of the term "bipolar disorder." When a person had a problem, we dealt with it the best way we could without whining or complaining. So when Vincent and I argued, I simply took it in stride. Although my parents were kind and loving to each other throughout their marriage, the same had not been the case for some of my aunts and uncles. Yes, they had stayed together for forty, fifty, and sixty or more years even though they could hardly stand each other. The love may have left their marriage entirely, but they never seemed to consider divorce. No, I was from a family that persevered. We were not quitters.

Living with a Stranger

When Vincent was moody and irritable, I didn't really take it that seriously. Most times, I felt it was a phase that would eventually pass. We quarreled constantly, and almost anything could serve as the spark for his incendiary temper. When he wasn't angry, he was sul-len, depressed, or just plain difficult to live with. The sole exception seemed to be when we were studying or when we were at school. He didn't want me to visit my parents, see my friends, or talk to our neighbors. He was possessive of me and my time, suspicious of all, and increasingly jealous. He wanted me to be with him all of the time, yet he wouldn't speak to me or treat me well when I *was* around.

If I went to the store, to the hairdresser's, or to the laundromat, he would time me based on how long he thought the task should take. Heaven forbid if I got caught in a traffic jam or were delayed in any way. If I were a minute late, he would interrogate me like a trial lawyer addressing a criminal. He was quick and clever with words, and although I was innocent of any wrongdoing, he could always make me look and feel as if I were in the wrong and needed to be punished.

Because he isolated me from people, I never really understood that he was playing mind games with me. I simply wanted to please my husband, as impossible as that had become. No matter how hard I tried, the bar was always raised. Before long, I stopped trying.

High Speed Car Crash

One morning, as we were making the commute from the city to Cheyney, we began arguing as usual. I can't remember what started the argument, but I do know that he was extremely angry with me. I remember him yelling and screaming, accusing me of things that I hadn't done. Meanwhile, he was barreling down that road entirely too fast. I had tired of him brow-beating me constantly, and as I sat in the passenger's seat listening to him yell and complain, something triggered inside me. I screamed back at him at the top of my lungs, telling him to shut up. Initially, he was shocked, but he soon back-handed me hard across the face. Without thinking of what I was doing, I slapped him back as hard as I could.

Before I could process what had just taken place, we were physically fighting as we drove down the highway. I can only imagine what we must have looked like to other drivers that morning, but at the moment, that didn't matter. He tried to grab me by my hair and pull me, as he would sometimes do at home. When he reached for me, however, I ducked, and the car swerved off of the road. Vincent over-corrected, trying to bring the speeding vehicle back into its lane, and the car spun out of control. We rolled several times, and the car finally came to a stop on its roof. I remember my life flashing before my eyes. I was certain that we were going to die, and yet I wasn't afraid. As far as I was concerned, death would be a welcome respite from the hell in which I had been living.

We did not die. Actually, we weren't even hurt, but his green Impala, which he loved more than me, was utterly destroyed. The roof was only inches from the steering wheel, the windshield was crushed, and the doors were jammed shut. We managed to climb out of the side windows. Vincent emerged completely unscathed, and the only injury that I received was a small cut on my left knee and the embarrassment of having acted like a God-forsaken sinner.

God Gets Our Attention

Instantly, we realized that it was only by the providence of God that our lives had been spared. We looked at each other and recognized that though we had just climbed from the wreckage of a terrible accident, we had been blessed beyond measure. God had given us a chance to reconcile our marriage. The Lord Jesus Christ had sent His guardian angels to protect us that day because He had a plan and a purpose for both Vincent and me. I had always felt that the Lord had His hand on my life for a special reason, but I hadn't known what it was. After that accident, I vowed to the Lord that I would no longer fight or act like Vincent. I would strive to live like the Christian woman that God wanted me to be, even if it meant living with a difficult husband.

And the Lord was with Jan...

the "church" that wasn't a church: seeking help

Upon this rock I shall build my church.

Matthew 16:18 (KJV)

I realized that newlyweds had it difficult under the best of conditions, but with both of us attending school, commuting, and working, our situation was especially hopeless. Our marriage continued to deteriorate as I found myself either ignoring Vincent's mood swings or making excuses for him. I had heard that people adjusted to marriage differently, and I considered the possibility that it was taking Vincent a longer time to adjust to this very drastic change. He was a loner by nature, and perhaps sharing his life with someone and opening up to them was just going to take him more time than some.

Isolation and lack of a social life made things worse for me. It was very rare for Vincent to allow me to see my family or even to call my friends. This behavior was not just limited to me, however. He isolated himself from his own family who lived in Philly, as well. He felt that his mom and siblings didn't like or accept him, and while I don't believe that was true, his perception had become reality. While his family *did* love him, they were not as patient and accepting of him as they should have been—or at least that was my opinion. In retrospect, I understand that they were simply doing the best that they could, much like I was.

You Always Hurt the Ones You Love

One evening Vincent and I had an explosive argument. He began pushing me around, and I had finally had enough of his abuse. I balled up my fist, socked him in his mouth, and ran out of our apartment as fast as I could with Vincent following close behind. How long I ran, I don't remember. I just ran like the wind.

I didn't know where to go or what to do. It was getting dark and cold, and I was becoming desperate. Still, I continued running, too scared even to look back to see if Vincent were still chasing me.

Store Front Church

I don't remember how long I ran, but I soon heard music and the sound of women's voices coming from a building. Looking up, I determined that the singing was coming from a small storefront church. Many inner-city churches were located in homes or rented storefronts since small congregations often could not afford an actual church building. My heart leapt for joy when I realized what I had stumbled upon. It was as if the Lord's guardian angels had led me to a safe haven. Frantically, I opened the door and yelled, "Help! My husband is trying to hurt me!"

Roughly a dozen women in the room, most of them older, looked toward the door, startled. Some were standing by the communion table near the pulpit, while a few others were seated in the pews. All were dressed in somber clothing and looked like missionaries that one might see in magazine articles. They had been praying when I entered, but my cry for help had shattered the reverent atmosphere. No one said a word. They looked mortified, and I began to wonder whether I really had come to the right place. Sure, I might have looked a little strange with no coat, mussed hair and eyes wide with fright, but still—something wasn't right.

I can recall the scene vividly. The church was a large, open room, with a potbelly stove in the corner. Someone had done a wonderful job converting the building to look just like a conventional church, but it was just much smaller. There was even a pulpit high above the pews and a choir stand with two rows of chairs.

Even though the setting should have been a comfortable one, I couldn't shake the feeling that something was very wrong. I thought, *Why aren't they welcoming me in?* Then it struck me—appearing as I had, they probably thought I was a lunatic or a drunk. This being the late fifties, drugs were not yet the serious problem that they are today, and my panicked arrival would have seemed a little strange, even in the inner-city. Silently, the women continued staring at me, not moving a step. What was wrong with them? Couldn't they see that I needed help?

"Church Folks"

Trying to grasp what was happening, I cried out again, "My husband is trying to hurt me. Please help me!" I figured that perhaps the problem was that they didn't know me and didn't think I was serious. Still the frigid, old women stood rooted, not saying a word. None asked my name or what was wrong, and I could see that they were not going to help me.

In bewilderment, I looked into the eyes of those church folk, and what I saw scared me more than anything that Vincent could throw at me. They were not true believers at all, and they were most certainly not Christians. They looked at me with ridicule, rejection, and condemnation, and their eyes revealed all that was in their hearts. The message was perfectly clear, "You got yourself into this mess! Don't think that we are going to get involved. Now get out of here!"

How naive I had been! Because they looked like mothers and grandmothers—missionaries, even— I assumed they were wise and would help me. For a moment, I had even felt safe and secure, just waiting for one of them to take me into her arms and tell me that everything would be all right. This was a church, wasn't it? I knew that Scripture had reminded older women of their duty to teach and care for their younger sisters. These women, however, had never gotten that message. Their glares directed me to the door, and I numbly made my way out of the church and away from that den of callous "Christians."

Returning to the Familiar

I guess I just didn't understand people. The coldness of their response shocked me so badly that I decided to head back to my apartment. It was better to brave a crazed husband than a "church" full of cold, indifferent souls that wouldn't even ask my name. By the time I returned, Vincent was glad to see me. His moods were always shifting like that. We made up, but the experience of the "church" that wasn't would stay with me for years.

But the Lord was with Jan...

a serious cry
for help

Call upon me, and I will answer thee, and shew thee great and mighty things, which thou knowest not.

Jeremiah 33:3 (KJV)

Manipulative and Controlling

By nature, Vincent was a loner, and he never really wanted to go anywhere with me... or with anybody else, for that matter. Being around people made him nervous, so he wanted me to choose to stay at home with him. He was extremely jealous and would often accuse me of being unfaithful. He watched me like a hawk and would interrogate me about my whereabouts to see if my story changed in any way. He was adept at playing with my mind and skillful at manipulating situations to his own advantage. He had the ability to make himself look good while making me look like the angry and unreasonable person with a serious problem.

One Saturday afternoon, Vincent and I had completed our exam studies in our apartment, and I wanted him to take me to a movie. It was one of those rare times when we had been having a great time together, so I wanted to get out of the house and spend some quality time with him. Suddenly, right out of the blue, Vincent's mood changed from light-heartedness and glee to gloom and doom. Oh, how gullible I was. I didn't realize that Vincent was deliberately creating his moods swings to manipulate me. We ended up in a heated discussion that led to a shouting match. I had fallen into the very trap he had set for me. He made it look as if I had said something he didn't like, but he never wanted to go to the movies with me in the first place. To emphasize the point, he back-handed me across the face. I, in turn, slapped him back as hard as I could, and then "it was on."

A Call to the Police for Help

We were arguing, hitting, yelling, and banging doors so loudly that the entire neighborhood could hear us. I don't know which neighbor it was, but I thank God that one probably feared for my safety and called the police. The next thing I remember is hearing a loud knock at the front door and a deep male voice saying, "Open up! This is the police!" When I heard who it was, I was thrilled! My heart leaped for joy! Finally, I was going to get some help and protection and justice.

Bipolar and Clever

Both Vincent and I raced down the steps from our second floor apartment, but Vincent beat me to the door. He gingerly opened it, as if nothing had happened and thanked the officer for coming, Vincent slipped into his professional voice mode. He first apologized for the loud noises and then proceeded to calmly and articulately explain "his side of the situation." First, he asked the officer if he were a married man. The police officer answered, "Yes." Vincent then began explaining to this male officer that his wife was having one of her "female spells" during her "cycle." He said, "Man, it's that time of the month. You know how hysterical, irrational, and unreasonable they can be. I am sure you have had to deal with the same kind of situation at home. Can't women frustrate you with their temperamental behavior and unreasonableness during those times of the month? There is absolutely nothing a husband can do to please them. It's funny, but you can't live with them, and you can't live without them."

The naïve police officer and this bipolar, conniving, manipulative husband of mine were standing at my front door talking about me as if I were not even present! All the time Vincent was talking, this credulous police officer was nodding his head in complete agreement with everything he was saying. I wanted to scream. I couldn't believe my ears. Vincent went on to say to the officer, "I just wanted to talk to you man-to-man because I knew you could understand and identify with what I am going through."

The Absurdity of It All

To make matters worse, Vincent winked his eye at this gullible, unsuspecting, policeman. The officer smiled, winked back, and said, "Man, I sure do understand, but just keep the noise level down, please. You are upsetting your neighbors, and it doesn't look good for you."

I couldn't believe my eyes or ears. All the while I was standing there at this ridiculous scene, I felt as if I were having some horrible nightmare from which I couldn't shake myself awake. To put the icing on the cake, after the officer talked with Vincent, he turned to leave without ever addressing me to get my side to the story. That's when I completely flipped out. Shocked beyond belief at what had just happened, I began shrieking like a wild woman. "What kind of police officer are you anyway? How can you just hear one side of the situation? Aren't you going to do something to him for what he is doing to me? He needs to be arrested for hitting me! Don't tell me you are just going to listen to him and not do anything! I demand to talk to your supervisor!"

I was so upset by this time that I was yelling at that police officer like a crazy, demented fool who needed to be placed in a straight jacket, but I didn't care! I was upset, and I felt I had not received my fair share of justice.

Then the truly unbelievable happened. That police officer slowly turned back around, looked me squarely in the face, and told me in no uncertain terms, "Lady, if you don't lower your voice and get control of yourself in a hurry, I am going to have to arrest you and take you downtown for disturbing the peace!"

I almost fainted from hearing his reprimand. As the officer stood there on the steps scolding me, I turned to look at Vincent. He stood there calmly looking like the model of virtue. He was actually portraying a frustrated husband who had to live with an irate, enraged, and demented spouse while I was looking and acting like an insane idiot. His act was so convincing, I would have given him an Oscar myself.

As I reflect on the events of that particular day, it shames me to realize that I was not living up to who I was in Jesus Christ. Vincent behaved better than I, who was a child of the King. What had happened to me? Why had I not applied biblical principles to direct my life with wisdom and discernment? Why had I fallen prey to Vincent's mental manipulations? By now, I was so depressed and humiliated that I didn't know what to do. I realized that I could never depend on "the law" to assist me because the majority of the representatives of the law in the late fifties and early sixties were men. They couldn't or chose not to understand my plight.

A New Approach, but No Solution

At that moment I decided to make an appointment with my pastor. Reverend E.B. Roberts was a good man, a godly man, an understanding man, but he was a naïve man. Either he had no earthly idea what I was talking to him about, or he felt I was a young, emotional, and dramatic woman who blew all circumstances out of proportion. My reason for saying this is simple. Although Pastor Roberts listened patiently without interruption as I explained my situation to him, he never gave me good advice about how to handle my problem. In essence, he simply said that I needed to go back home, be more submissive to my husband, and try harder to be a better wife. Yes, my pastor went through the motions of listening and "being there" for his parishioner, but he neither addressed my problem nor believed that my dilemma was as serious as I had made it out to be. In my opinion, my pastor did not understand domestic violence. I now found myself in a precarious and very dangerous situation. The police didn't want to help me, and my pastor didn't know how to help me. I was in a mess.

But the Lord was with Jan...

the pursuit
and
realization
of a dream

For I know the thoughts that I think toward you, saith the LORD, thoughts of peace, and not of evil, to give you an expected end

Jeremiah 29:11

God has a weird sense of humor. No matter how hard we plan, things don't always turn out the way we expect them to.

Continuing to Struggle in School

Vincent and I were still working our way through college, and our marital problems had not improved; however, my grades were actually better than ever. For all of his other faults, Vincent was actually a great instructor, and he had the ability to explain, simplify, and reduce complex concepts down to something that even a youngster could understand. Because of his academic guidance, I became an outstanding student, and my grades improved significantly. Both of us were on the dean's list. My college assignments were no longer difficult for me, and I even began to enjoy learning.

The Quandary

One thing that continued to cause me anxiety, however, was the possibility that I might get pregnant before graduation. Throughout my childhood, my father had stressed the importance of "getting that piece of paper"—my diploma. Although my dad had never expressed his feelings, I had sensed his disappointment when I married before finishing college. He continued to be gracious, loving, and supportive of me (that was the kind of person he was), but I think that he felt I would never reach my goal, which was also his long-standing dream. I desperately wanted to prove to him that he was wrong—that I would finish on schedule and become the first member of my family to graduate from college. More than that, I wanted to give him a sense of pride and accomplishment. But I also believed that if I ever dropped out of college because of pregnancy or for some other reason, I would never return. It was an all-or-nothing proposition for me, and so my desire blossomed into an obsession of sorts.

Probing for Answers

However, delaying pregnancy was more like postponing the inevitable. During the late fifties and early sixties, contraceptive options were not what they are today. My mother couldn't help me because she didn't have any answer either. I could forget asking any of my girlfriends for advice, as they were just as ignorant as I was about sexual matters. My sister-in-law explained what had worked for her, though. Both of her children had been planned five years apart. I took her advice and used the rhythm method (which was based upon tracking my "fertile days"), along with a rubber diaphragm and some nasty jelly. It was awful!

Vincent and I were determined to postpone having a child until after graduation. We took all the precautions in our efforts to be responsible, but there was no room for tenderness or spontaneity with this method. Just preparing to "come together" took all of the romance out of intimacy, but we had one goal in mind—graduating on time. One can only imagine how much this affected our relationship. As complicated and unappealing as this method was, it still wasn't fool-proof. Every month, I was a nervous wreck until my cycle would start. It's hard to believe that people actually lived like this, but we did. Though we did everything we could to avoid getting pregnant before graduation, it happened anyway. When I later held my diaphragm up to the light to check it, I could see a tiny hole at the corner of the rim that I had not seen earlier.

Asking for the Impossible

We humans map out our own paths, but ultimately, God's plans always supersede ours. When I realized I was pregnant, I was shocked and devastated. Yes, there are many women who would have been thrilled to be in my shoes, but that didn't make me feel any better. To me, it was similar to the time when I was little and didn't want to clean my plate at dinner time. My mom would tell me about all the children starving in China and how they would love to have my leftovers. I always thought to myself, "Fine! I'll mail it to them." Just because someone else would be happy with my situation didn't mean that I was.

I continued to pout and fret, and it was a while before I did what I should have done in the first place— *pray*! Since God obviously wanted me to have a baby at this particular time in my life, and because nothing is impossible with Him, I prayed for a miracle. I prayed to God that I would not "show" until graduation day. I was student teaching at the time, and in those days, married teachers were not allowed to teach beyond her third month. But she would have to leave earlier if it became obvious that she was pregnant. A teacher could not look like she was "with child" in front of the students.

My situation was complicated by the fact that I was so painfully thin and weighed only ninety-two pounds. But God showed Himself omnipotent by enabling me to remain reasonably flat throughout my student teaching practicum and allowing me to graduate on time with no harm to my baby. What an answer to my prayer! I had not one single sick day through my pregnancy and was able to go to school each day. It was a marvelous time in my life.

The conclusion to this episode was even more amazing. On the day of my graduation, my body changed. I blew up like a balloon, and there was absolutely no more hiding that I was pregnant, but it didn't matter at that point. I had made it. On May 29, 1961, in full view of my family and the world, I proudly walked across that commencement stage in my cap and gown to receive my Bachelor of Science Degree in Elementary Education from the president of Cheyney State Teachers' College. It was the happiest day of my life. Dad was thrilled. God had answered my prayer beyond my hopes and expectations.

As proud as they were at my graduation, my mom and dad were even more proud three months later. On August 14, my gift from the Lord was born—my parent's precious grandson, Dexter. He was a healthy baby, weighing in at six pounds, fifteen ounces, and measuring twenty-one inches long. He was ordained by God for a divine purpose, and even though he didn't know it, he had attended college and a graduation before he was even born. What a joy!

God's Humor is Our Delight!

I remain convinced God has a hilarious sense of humor. Though there was a great deal of anxiety and concern during the pregnancy, we all laughed after it was over. Dexter, my baby boy, was born in God's time, not mine, and His timing is always perfect.

And the Lord was with Jan...

seeking shelter in a domestic storm

> For in the time of trouble He shall hide me in his pavilion: in the secret of His tabernacle shall He hide me; He shall set me up upon a rock.
>
> Psalm 27:5 (KJV)

I felt like a child on the playground, sitting on a see-saw with a big bully harassing me. But a child could run home from the playground to the safety and security of his parents. I was already home, and there was no safety or security for me or my child.

Something Had to Give

Vincent was a truly miserable human being, and he was turning both my son and me into the same. As an insecure man who could not cope with his emotions, Vincent was being forced to face his greatest fear—losing his son and me; yet everything that he did pushed us apart. I walked on egg shells, always afraid of saying or doing something to trigger an angry reaction from him. The anxiety was beginning to take a toll on my physical and emotional health. Here I was, a young married woman with my precious child, and my husband was victimizing both of us. We couldn't talk as normal husbands and wives do because he would inevitably accuse me of being against him or blame me for his violent tirades. After so much of this, I actually began to believe that our insufferable marriage really was my fault.

What Do You Do When You Don't Know What to Do?

Leaving was a given, but at the moment, I had no place to go. I was living in Gary, Indiana, more than a thousand miles away from my parents in Philly, and just coping with Vincent's terrorizing behavior had kept me from making any close friends locally. I didn't even know of any neighbors that I could talk to or confide in. Vincent's hostility and lack of socialization had kept me isolated from others, and there were no shelters for battered women and children as we know them today, or at least none that I was aware of. Women in my predicament needed to learn how to cope and make the best out of a bad situation.

To make matters worse, I was penniless. I had not begun my teaching career yet because it was cheaper for me to stay at home and care for my baby and live off of Vincent's meager salary than to try to hire a babysitter. I loved being a stay at home wife and mother, but I hated the way Vincent treated me and his child. It wasn't right, and living in constant fear and depression was beginning to take its toll on my health-mentally and physically. In an effort to change Vincent's behavior and make him more appreciative of me and his child, I began making plans to leave him temporarily and check into a bed and bath in a downtown area of Gary. I began scrapping together all of the loose change I could find around the house in order to get away, even if it were only for one night. I wanted to make my husband miss us and then lovingly take us back. The loose coins I found did not add up to much, but for me, they were like pennies from heaven—they were enough to buy me an escape, even if it was just for one day or two. Vincent always collected the change in his pockets each evening and placed it in a jar. I added those coins, as well, and before long, I had enough money for a room at a bed and breakfast.

Beginning to Have a Little Backbone

I didn't know where to go, so I began calling places listed in the phone book. After calling several places and inquiring about their prices, I decided to stay at the Dolly Madison Bed and Breakfast downtown Gary over night or a few days. I called to make reservations for my baby and me. The lady that answered the phone sounded warm and very maternal, assuring me that there were plenty of comfortable rooms available. She even told me that she would make sure that there would be a crib set up for my son. Excitedly, I threw a few necessities into a piece of luggage for Dexter and me. On the table was a note for Vincent, telling him where we would be.

This Can't Really Be Happening

After catching a cab to take us across town, I entered the lobby of the inn and was met by the lady who had made my reservation. A stunned look registered on her face, and her voice turned harsh and cold. It was nothing like the warm, inviting voice I had heard earlier. She made no effort to conceal her disdain for me, and I knew that the color of my skin was the reason for the abrupt change in her attitude. Her next words confirmed it, "I did not realize that you were 'colored' when I spoke with you on the phone. All the rooms are taken. I have no vacancies. Sorry!"

I couldn't believe my ears. What was I to do? I couldn't go back home, and now this woman would not let me stay. Dr. King was fighting for the dignity of us living in the South, but this was Gary, Indiana… in the North… in 1961. Surely this was not happening, but it was. I was paralyzed with disappointment and rejection. The proprietor of this establishment was denying me a place to stay solely because of the color of my skin.

Taking a Non-Verbal Stand

Unable to hide my anger and humiliation, I could feel tears well up in my eyes and roll down my cheeks. In that moment, I decided that I did not want this woman to see how badly she had hurt my child and me, so I prayed silently and stood my ground. Our eyes locked, and both of us did not flinch in the slightest. We just glared at each other. I never said a word, and I did not move, not knowing what she might do next. She could call the police and have me arrested, or maybe she would throw me out herself, or maybe she would give me a room. She had lots of options, but I had none. However, no matter what she did, I was not going back to where I was running from.

Her icy gaze remained on me, and I wondered if this standoff might last all night. How much time passed as the two of us stood glaring at each other, I don't really know. But finally she had a change of mind and backed down a little. She smiled slightly and changed her attitude toward me. Her next words were so kind that they brought joy to my heart and tears to my eyes. She said, "I was mistaken. I think I do have one back room left, if you still want it."

Answered Prayer

I realize now that it was nothing but the Lord pulling on her heart strings. Prayer always works. The Lord allowed her to look beyond the color of my skin and see a desperate and frightened mother with her baby standing before her.

Gratefully, I accepted the room and paid for it and my cab fare with the coins that I had worked so hard to save. I was so relieved to be free of my home. To me, prejudice was a piece of cake compared to the hostile environment my son and I had endured at home.

The room was small and nondescript, but it was clean, comfortable, and peaceful. I changed Dexter, fed him, and laid him down on my bed to sleep. He was such a good baby, and he had never fussed or cried like most babies do. I was very thankful to God for this blessing because I don't think that I could have handled a fussy baby at this point in my life.

Business Not as Usual

Needless to say, when Vincent arrived home from school that day and did not find his dinner waiting for him, he was upset, to say the least. He immediately called the number I had left by the phone, ranting and raving about my running away. Without a trace of anxiety, I told him that he would never see Dexter or me again if he didn't change how he treated us.

Vincent slammed down the receiver, but I was hardly surprised when he called back several minutes later with a different tone and attitude. Eventually, he came to pick us up, and his behavior improved for a while. It wasn't for very long, though—it never was. Can a leopard change its spots? Absolutely not! Still, I had taken the first step toward being less of a victim. God was working within me to change my thinking. I was living

Romans 12:2, "Be not conformed to this world; but be ye transformed by the renewing of your mind."

I needed to change my frame of mind because it was making me a prisoner. It had me locked in a stronghold. Could our marriage be saved? Would he change for the better?

Only time would tell.

"And the Lord was with Jan..."

transitioning from college, work, and beyond

Be not conformed to this world; but be ye transformed by the renewing of your mind.

Romans 12:2 (KJV)

Model Employee, Mediocre Family Man

After relocating from Philadelphia to Gary, I remained at home most of my son's first year in order to be a full time wife and mother. Though I enjoyed my new role, we were stretched to the limit financially, living on Vincent's salary alone. I wanted to take on a job, but I first needed a babysitter for our son. I soon found a grandmotherly neighbor to take care of Dexter. I accepted a second grade teaching position and officially joined the teaching staff at Jefferson Elementary School. My principal, Mrs. Gertrude Ward, was an older, caring administrator, and we bonded almost instantly. I was a model teacher because of the great education I had received at Cheyney University.

In September of 1964, our second son Lawrence was born. He joined Dexter as the greatest joy of my life; however, Vincent did not appear to enjoy this new blessing as much as I did. He remained unfulfilled with a restlessness and discontentment that colored his attitude toward everything around him. At home, Vincent's routine verbal abuse continued. He was temperamental and impatient with his sons and with me. Our well-being was deteriorating in the face of constant stress and fear brought on by Vincent's volatile temper. I never invited anyone to our home since I never knew exactly what would set him off. This worked out surprisingly well but only because Vincent was a loner by nature, so he never wanted company anyway. We lived a thousand miles from Philadelphia, so the boys and I were isolated from the ones who cared for us the most. My boys visited their friends and were welcomed in their homes and were nurtured by other parents, church folks, and neighbors.

In order to bring harmony to the lives of my two sons and me, I centered my life around the Lord and my job. I realized that I could not change Vincent, but I did have the power to change our thinking. I began to reflect upon the principles that I was learning in the Word of God. Slowly, my thoughts were brought under the control of God. I would first seek the kingdom of God and His righteousness and not conform to Vincent's warped view of life. Through Jesus Christ, I would use positive thoughts to transform our minds and our lives. Our neighbors and fellow church members thought of the boys and me as the three musketeers, but Christ was always with us. We went to church, the barbershop, the grocery store, the library, movies, museums, the zoo, relatives' homes out of state, sport events—you name it, we did it. This difficult time helped to show me that life really is what one chooses to make of it.

A Strong, Positive Trait

Vincent did have one strong virtue—his work ethic. I can't remember him missing a single day in nearly twenty years. Additionally, he was an excellent provider. I knew of many husbands who treated their wives well but squandered the money or hoarded it for themselves. Vincent gave me his entire paycheck for as long as we were married. I gave him an agreed-upon allowance, and he entrusted the rest of the money to me for managing the household. He was a model employee and a leader outside the home, making it even more sad that he had turned his home into a place of misery.

Habitually Predictable

As our sons grew older, Vincent's erratic home behavior grew more insufferable. He continued to live like a hermit, and seldom (if ever) did he communicate with his family back in Philly. He had no friends at work and did not seem to want any. More tellingly, he did not interact with us, his immediate family. Vincent never took us anywhere, did anything for us or with us, or included us in his personal life. It was as if we did not exist. Every Friday and Saturday night, he would dress up and go to the bars, leaving his family at home. He would sometimes stay out all night and return after the sun had come up the next day. Although his behavior set a bad example for our sons, it was a time of peace and tranquility for us. In a sad way, we came to look forward to our reprieve each weekend.

Graduate School and Administrative Promotions

In 1966, Vincent returned to school to work on his master's degree in administration and supervision. He graduated in 1968 but did not attend his graduation ceremony. Later, he was appointed principal of Banneker Elementary School. Over the next year, I completed my degree in administration. I begged Vincent to attend my graduation ceremony and to bring our sons with him, but he refused. As usual, I left the antisocial Vincent at home and took my sons with me. Family members of one of my friends who was also graduating agreed to let Dexter and Lawrence sit with them during the graduation ceremony. That meant I had to entrust my sons to complete strangers as I walked across the stage to receive my degree. I could hear their precious voices shouting, "We love you, Mommy!" and "Hey, hey, Mommy!" as I walked across the stage. They were proud of me, and I was as happy as could be. Once again, the Lord had come through for us. Afterward, the three of us went out for Chinese food at one of our favorite restaurants. Because I was such a regular, Jimmy Wong, the owner, treated us to a free dinner as a graduation gift to me. What a blessing!

Married to My Job

After graduation, I applied for the Superintendent's Administrative Internship Academy and was accepted. Upon completion in 1972, I served as assistant principal and a year later was appointed principal of John H. Vohr Elementary School. At that point, my job became my sanctuary. Whether working in the classroom or as principal, I could always escape the drama at home with Vincent and be my true self.

Because I worked such long hours and took pride in everything I did, people thought of me as a dedicated worker (to the point of even calling me a workaholic, in some cases). Yes, I did have a strong work ethic. Discipline and hard work had been instilled in me by my parents and teachers, but there was more than just that. I worked hard for two other reasons. One was that the only place I could gain the recognition I so desperately craved was at work. Doing a good job gave me a sense of significance. But the second reason—and the bigger factor—was that it was more pleasant at work than at home. It is sad, but my sons and I never found what we needed to make us feel whole at home. When I became a principal, Dexter and Lawrence hung out at school, playing basketball in the gym while I finished paperwork in my office. I could hear them play, and they could communicate with me, using the intercom system. Even though I worked long hours, my sons were happy to stay at school with me, even on the weekends. Often, their friends would join them after school and on the weekends to play basketball and have fun in the gym. My sons were finally able to socialize and have fun—something that they could never do in our home. So it was only natural that I loved work.

Did I realize that my situation wasn't normal? Yes, I knew that most people felt the opposite, that work was to make a living and that home was where the heart is, but I accepted my way of life and dealt with it the only way that I knew how. Consequently, I enjoyed being the principal of John H. Vohr Elementary School, and the Lord enabled me to excel.

My school's enrollment was approximately seven hundred and thirty students, but I had no assistant principal. I had a staff of eighty-two—teachers, teacher-aides, office workers, custodians, and food staff personnel. We were like a family, and I was also blessed with a wonderfully supportive group of parents. Serving as principal during the '70s was far different from today. That was before the time of state and federally mandated testing and "No Child Left Behind." Children learned at their own pace, and teachers had time to teach the material. Students learned the basics of reading, writing, and arithmetic, and they were not asked to rush through a curriculum designed by those who knew nothing about them. I enjoyed what I did, and working in this nurturing environment helped me to keep my sanity during my long marital nightmare.

"And the Lord was with Jan..."

the paradoxical plight of the married-single

Then the Lord God said, "It is not good that man should be alone. I will make a helper who is right for him."

Genesis 2:18 (KJV)

Definition of a Married-Single

Before long, I had become what I classify as a "married single." Married singles are legally bound to a mate by a marriage license, but that's as far as it goes. Their vows are just words devoid of meaning. The couple may live under the same roof, and they may even sleep together in the same bed and share the same bank accounts, but their lives are completely separate. The married singles usually enter this nebulous condition either by convenience or neglect of the relationship.

For all practical purposes in lives of married singles, there is no love, no true emotion, and no relationship. The marriage represents a legally binding contract, and there is no mutual feeling of belonging. Many times, the marriage is purely platonic. The darker side of this relationship is the isolation and rejection felt by one or both of the individuals involved.

Uniquely Unexceptional

While one might think married singles are rare, they are actually quite common. This arrangement is often tolerated because society assumes that people are most able to serve in certain capacities if they are married. Politicians are a great example of this misguided thinking. Only in a few cases does our nation choose an unmarried candidate over a married one for any high-profile office. CEOs and pastors of churches are other examples of positions that practically demand one be married.

In most instances, it is believed that a person is more stable if he or she is married. What we overlook is that remaining single is better than enduring misery and mistreatment.

The Grass Is Greener Syndrome

With so many married singles evident in our society, one would think that singles would appreciate their freedom and that they would relax until God sends them their partner. I suppose it's true that marriage with the right partner can be heaven on earth, but I never found out. God ordained marriage, so it was meant to be good. Everything that God made *is* good. Men and women have made a mess of things. It is human nature to be dissatisfied with the status quo, and man will always want what he doesn't (or can't) have.

Not Easily Detectable or Discernable

Married-singles have learned to disguise their emptiness and loneliness quite well. They put up a convincing front and pride themselves at being able to fool everyone. I know because I mastered the game. I wanted a real marriage—one with warmth and intimacy. It just didn't turn out that way.

It's strange to me (and it would be hilarious were it not such a serious matter) that there are so many single women who would "give anything" to be married. They are fixated on getting a man just for the sake of being married. If they only knew how many married singles envy them, they would reconsider. I would certainly have given them Vincent, if I could have.

God's Promises, Providence, and Presence for This Married "Single" Mom

Realizing my plight as a married single, I turned to God for wisdom and direction. I could not control Vincent, but I had the power to change my thinking. I began to dwell on the principles that I was learning in the Word of God, and my thoughts were brought under the control of God.

First, I would seek the kingdom of God and His righteousness. I would no longer conform to Vincent's warped thinking. My sons and I would transform our minds through Jesus Christ... The Lord was with us. I wanted to make happy childhood memories for my children, and I wanted them to realize that even if circumstances are far less than perfect, we *always* have the power to make the best of a bad situation.

"And the Lord was with Jan..."

how I came to study the bible

Study to shew thyself approved unto God.

2 Timothy 2:15 (KJV)

Although I had been saved at the age of nine in Vacation Bible School in 1949, no one told me that I needed to be baptized until much later. In Sunday school, I learned that Jesus had been baptized in the Jordan River by John the Baptist and that even though baptism alone would not save me, it would serve to announce to the world that I was a born again believer in Jesus Christ. Therefore, on Easter Sunday in the spring of 1952, I was baptized at the age of twelve. It was a glorious experience.

At that age, I could not possibly have understood that salvation would save me spiritually from eternal damnation or that my study of the Bible would save me physically and emotionally in both of my turbulent marriages. God works in mysterious ways. But I am getting ahead of myself. Let's start at the beginning.

Neighborhood Bible Teacher

When I was still in elementary schools, Mrs. Elaine Lemon lived in my neighborhood, and to this day I am convinced that she was an angel. She was married to a kind and gentle man, and together they took it upon themselves to invite us rough (and occasionally ungrateful) neighborhood youngsters into their home to study the Bible. This wonderful couple never had children, but during those Monday afterschool Bible study sessions, they treated us as if we were their own. Mrs. Lemon was the teacher, but Mr. Lemon supported her quietly from the background. He never spoke a word, or at least not that I can remember.

Mrs. Lemon stressed Scripture memorization, and one verse that she insisted we all learn was 2 Timothy 2:15, "Study to shew thyself approved unto God, a workman that needeth not to be ashamed, rightly dividing the word of truth." To this day, I remember that verse. I suppose that if I ever suffered amnesia, I would still be able to quote it; that's how much Mrs. Lemon engraved that particular verse into my young mind.

Beginning to Drift from Biblical Teachings

My studies with Mrs. Lemon continued during elementary and junior high school, but I dropped out of Mrs. Lemon's Bible class when I entered high school. Why? I don't know. I just lost interest, I suppose. Not only did I stop attending Bible classes, but I also stopped reading my Bible on my own. I was involved in extracurricular activities in high school, and before long, other interests began to crowd out my love for the Lord.

In those days, the preachers at Holy Temple Church would stand behind the pulpit, read a verse or two, give a sermon title, close the Bible, and begin talking. At least, that is the way I remember it. I think most church services were conducted that way, with not a lot of biblical teaching from the pulpit. People were shouted at or entertained—but not taught. The preachers would hoot and holler as the congregation would stand and respond with loud "Amens" or "Hallelujahs." The Bible was rarely used as a point of reference, and since the preacher didn't seem to value the word of God, it became less important to me, as well.

To make matters worse, the sermons never made much sense to my friends or me. We all went to church together, but it had never dawned upon us that the sermons were actually Bible based and could help us if we applied them to our lives. As a result, the music for us became the most important part of the church service. The choir and musical instruments were the highlight of our worship experience.

Between Sunday school and church services, we would go downstairs to the basement to buy slices of delicious cake and sweet potato pie. I rarely had enough money to purchase dessert, but some of my friends did, and they would share with me.

That was the gist of church as a teenager. Even though I had been saved and accepted Jesus Christ years earlier, I still didn't fully understand what worship was all about, and no one took the time to explain it to me. I simply did what I saw most adults doing at the time.

Driven Back to the Word of God

After years with Vincent, I had become so miserable that desperation drove me to the Bible. I played what might be called the game of "Bible Roulette," where I would open my Bible and read whatever page I happened to come upon. I needed answers to help me endure my horrible life, but of course I could not find what I needed using such a haphazard approach. Eventually, I became even more frustrated.

One day, I was commuting to Chicago from Gary, as I usually did during the summer months as I worked toward my master's degree. Since I rode the same train each morning and evening, I would see the same conductor, and it was not long before we would strike up a conversation as he punched my ticket each day. One topic led to another, and eventually the conversation turned to the latest best-selling novels, and then the Bible. Jack asked me if I had ever read the Bible in its entirety.

When I told him that I hadn't, he told me of a book he had once read, about a young boy who idolized his father, a brilliant, successful business man. Unfortunately, the man's son was nothing like his father; and since he was moderately retarded, he failed in school. Consequently, this man's son became a great disappointment and embarrassment to him. The more the boy tried to please his father, the worse things became. Nothing worked.

One day, an older grandfatherly figure in the neighborhood took pity on this young boy and began to talk with him. The older man suggested that if he wanted to get good grades in school, he should use the Bible to help him. He recommended that the boy study the questions for his test then put the questions and the Bible under his pillow and sleep on them all night. Amazingly, it worked. The boy continued this routine, and before long, his grades improved, and so did his relationship with his father.

New Determination to Study the Word of God

After listening to Jack's story (interrupted several times, as he collected fares and punched train tickets), it dawned on me that I had just been given a "rare jewel." I am not sure if the story was true, but I knew I would never forget it. The story made me think to myself, "What would happen if I purposed in my heart to begin to study my Bible consistently and diligently?" Maybe the word of God would give me the wisdom I needed to change my miserable marriage and otherwise sad life. Right then and there, sitting on the South Shore Commuter Train one summer day in 1970, I rededicated myself to the Lord. I would read one to three chapters each day until God took me home to be with Him.

My life was never the same after that day on that commuter train. I was refreshed and inspired, starting that very afternoon. I drove to my babysitter's home to pick up my two sons, who were being watched by an elderly church member. Then I went home, cooked dinner, fed my husband and sons, cleaned the kitchen, studied my lessons for my administrative and supervision classes, put my boys to bed, and began the adventure of reading the Bible in its entirety.

Different Approach to Bible Study

Although most people will tell new Bible students to begin their reading with the Gospel of John, that didn't make any sense to me. What other book in the world would one pick up and begin reading in the middle? How would I be able to make sense of what I was reading? So, I began my reading at Genesis 1:1, "In the beginning."

That was the summer of 1970. Today, I still read my Bible every evening.

Though I read like this for several years, I was still as uninformed as ever when it came to understanding God's Word. Something was missing. Yes, I knew facts, and whenever it came to Bible trivia, I was terrific. I knew all the answers to simple questions. But when it came to applying God's principles to my life and marriage, I was a total failure. It seemed I was reading more and learning less. Instead of feeling fulfilled and at peace, I felt agitated because I was still a dismal failure with my life. What was wrong with me? I decided to ask the Lord.

The Holy Spirit Won't Teach Imposters

After much prayer, the Lord let me know that the Bible is not a trophy to be used to make myself look good. I had been reading the Bible for the wrong reasons. Although I had begun for the right reasons without guidance and discipline, my motives had become impure. I immediately confessed my sin and repented. I claimed 1 John 1:9 and asked the Lord to help me. God is so good! I learned that I had a built-in spiritual tutor who would teach me and guide me as I studied the Bible if only I would ask: it was the third person of the Trinity, the Holy Spirit. He now guides me into all truth as a loving, patient, spiritual teacher.

After that revelation, I no longer read three chapters each night; instead, I read fewer chapters and studied more. I tried to read one chapter (or at least a few verses) in the morning before work to start my day off on the right foot. In the evenings I would read two chapters, if I could. But first, I would pray and ask the Lord to guide me, teach me, and help me apply what I needed to know. Each word, each phrase, and each verse was spoken by God, revealing more to me as I explored.

Life Was No longer the Same

At this point in my life, I was not the same woman who was reading the Bible just for show. I was reading my Bible consistently and prayerfully to get to know Him—the author and finisher of my faith. My thirst for knowing Him made me want to read and study even more. Finally, I began learning to apply and share what I was learning. As far as my marriage was concerned, I was learning to put everything in God's hand.

"And the Lord was with Jan..."

enough is enough

Then Jesus said to them, "That's enough!"

Luke 22:38 (KJV)

As I reflect on my life, I remember being taught to take vows seriously and keep my commitments. In my family, divorce was not an option. My parents and all my aunts and uncles celebrated their fiftieth wedding anniversaries. It was as natural as breathing. No one dared to even mention the "D" word. Even though life was difficult and they faced many struggles, they all stuck it out. As unhappy or discontented as they might have been, divorce was simply not an option for them. Commitment to their vows superseded any misery they might have felt, and they were in it for the long haul. That was how I was raised.

But enough is enough! There comes a time in each person's life when he must decide when he has had enough of something, whether that thing is a person, a situation, or even just an attitude. For me, the time came later rather than sooner. It took me nearly twenty years to realize that I did not have a marriage and, even more incredibly, I didn't come to this conclusion on my own. My reality check came through my two sons, Dexter and Lawrence.

Unsurprisingly Predictable Routine

During my many years with Vincent, I had come to realize that I could count on the unchanging routine of my family life. During the week, he would go to work and return home every evening. Every Friday and Saturday night, he would go out on the town—alone. He was so predictable, that you could mark it down on your calendar.

The Interruption

One particular Saturday evening, however, our entire routine changed. Dexter and Lawrence wanted to go out with friends of theirs from church. One of the mothers from around the block volunteered to take them along with a few other boys for dinner and a movie. It seemed like a great idea to me, but I didn't share this information with Vincent. I knew he would have said, "No," so I let my sons go without asking for their father's permission. They needed this outing; it would be good for them to get out and socialize with friends. I didn't really think that it would be much of an issue. Vincent was a creature of habit, and usually when he went out Saturday nights, he never made it back before the boys and I had left for Sunday School or church the following morning.

Much to my surprise, Vincent came home early that evening. I was flabbergasted! He got the surprise of his life too. When he realized that the boys were not at home, he blew his top and demanded to know where his sons were. I explained that they were out having fun with their church friends and a neighbor. I hoped that saying the word "church" would settle him some. Although Vincent never went to church with us, he had never stopped the rest of us from going. He seemed to get some comfort from the idea of church, yet he still claimed that all church goers were "hypocrites and jerks." His anger grew as he ranted and raved like a madman. Looking back, it was as if he wanted to work himself into a frenzy. He repeatedly asked me questions that I had already answered for him. Who were the boys with? Where were they at that very moment? When had they left? When would they return home? He was firing questions at me so fast that I couldn't think straight. All the while, he accused me of being an unfit mother, calling me every ugly name in the book.

Totally Embarrassed

Above Vincent's ranting, I thought I heard a car pull up outside. I silently prayed that it was my boys returning home. Thank God, it was. Watching her from the doorway, I could see my neighbor smiling unsuspectingly as she got out of her car. My sons were happy as well, and I could tell that they all had enjoyed their time out. I desperately wanted to alert her to what was happening, but she would not have understood. Like everyone else, she thought of us as a normal family. However, nothing that was about to happen was normal.

I was still positioned in the doorway as she escorted my sons back to the house. This sweet neighbor stood facing me, apologizing over and over again for keeping my boys out so late. She said that the movie was longer than they had expected, and she thought it would be fine with us since we knew that the boys were with her. The look in my eyes and my body language should have warned her of what was about to happen, but she didn't get the message. I couldn't blame her. Few could have understood this situation, unless they had lived with someone like Vincent.

Suddenly, Vincent lunged forward and verbally lashed out at her in anger. His violence left her speechless, and I will never forget the shocked and terrified expression on her face. She had never experienced anything so horrific in her life. For a moment, she remained paralyzed with fear. After regaining her composure, she turned and ran to her car as quickly as she could. I could hear her sobbing. For years, my boys and I had dreaded a scene like this. We knew that it was bound to happen one day, though, and that Saturday night it had. We knew what kind of person Vincent was, but it was something completely different to have others see it as well. We could no longer hide our family's shame.

Secretly, I wished that she would return with her husband, angry and ready to tear into Vincent for treating his wife like that. It never happened, though. I think the entire neighborhood considered him to be as dangerous as he was different and all avoided us.

The Last Straw

At this point, I knew there would be no use trying to make Vincent understand why I had allowed the boys to go out. Still, I tried to impress upon him that our sons needed to socialize with friends once in a while. Vincent was in one of his crazy moods, however, and he decided to vent the evening's frustrations upon me. We had an unspoken agreement never to argue in front of the boys. I never wanted them to witness the friction. How naïve I was. Children are quite perceptive and often sense what they may not actually see or hear.

This particular night was the last straw for Vincent. While I stood in front of him, talking, he swung his fist at me. I had no time to dodge his powerful blow. When his punch landed, it was so fierce that it left me seeing stars. I remember falling to the floor while my sons could only watch. I blacked out for a short time, and when I came to, I remember hearing my oldest son yelling at his dad and saying, "You better not hit my mommy again!" In my semi-conscious state, I couldn't see anything, but their voices rang out loudly and clearly. Vincent was so angry that he began to whip Dexter something terrible. I tried to get up and defend Dexter, but Vincent must have hit me again because everything went black.

The Wakeup Call

Later, my sons were there for me. They said, "Mom, we need to talk to you." They asked how I could be so wise in some things and yet so unwise in others?

"When it comes to your marriage, why can't you see that you don't have one? You tell us that you don't want to leave our dad because you don't want us coming from a broken family. Well, Mom, you need to know that we aren't a family! We are a wreck! It has always been broken. It's a mess! And Mom, we want you to know one more thing. If our dad ever puts his hands on you ever again, it is going to be him and us! You need to know that your sons are not going to stand by and see you hurt by him or anybody!"

Dexter told me how he had stood his ground with his father.

"I'm not scared any more. He whipped me, but I didn't cry or anything," he told me excitedly. At that moment, I realized that my son had passed from childhood to adulthood. Dexter had become a man of integrity, courage, and maturity, and Vincent knew it. He had humiliated himself in front of his own two sons, and they had seen him for what he really was—a bully. Vincent would never redeem himself in his sons' eyes. I was so proud of my sons. They had done for me what I couldn't do for myself.

Finally Coming to My Senses

My head had been buried in the sand for too long; those words of my children cut me deeper than any knife. It hurt me to realize the injustice and harm I had done to them. It was one thing for me to suffer, but it was another thing altogether to know that my children were suffering. No decent, loving mother could let that continue.

Enough was enough. Right then and there I begged the Lord to forgive me, to sustain me, and to give me the wisdom and strength to do what had to be done. At last I knew that I had to get a divorce. I had given him almost twenty years to change, and he still wasn't the husband and father he needed to be. We had experienced Vincent's violent temper for the last time.

And the Lord was with Jan...

PART TWO: divorced, marriage number two, and the ministry

transformed and moving out and on

And be not conformed to this world; but be ye transformed by the renewing of your mind.

Romans 12:2 (KJV)

The joy of the Lord is your strength.

Nehemiah 8:10 (KJV)

A Major Decision

For years, my children and I had walked on eggshells and were terrorized by the thought of Vincent's exploding in anger. For years, we had been bound by these invisible chains. But that was all about to change. I was transformed, not reformed—I changed spiritually from the inside out. It was instantaneous. I was no longer intimidated by Vincent. Best of all, I was a new person.

My day of transformation and self-determination came when I decided to end the charade of a marriage to Vincent and move out. My sons immediately recognized the difference in me. They didn't know what had happened to me, but they both liked what they saw. My newfound strength encouraged my children, even though Vincent didn't notice anything different. That was nothing out of the ordinary; he never really took notice of me or his sons. For once, his inattentiveness was a good thing, especially since it would help me develop my "get-away" plans. It would serve him right.

Planning and Preparing to Move

My awareness of God's presence was awesome. It changed my outlook on life. Old things had become new for me. This spiritual transformation was not only therapeutic, but it was uplifting, as well. I took great pleasure in stealthily formulating my exodus. I could visualize our freedom. My plans became an obsession with me once I began to realize that the days of living in misery were about to end.

I needed a viable plan and strategy. I couldn't afford to jump out of the proverbial frying pan into the fire. The three of us were going to need a place to live, as well as furniture, movers, and everything else that goes along with moving. Never before had our future looked so bright. Still, I was cautious not to let Vincent suspect anything. It was in his nature to be suspicious of everything and everybody, so I did not tell my two sons of my plans right away. Why not? They were young and innocent, and I didn't want them to have to carry this burden in the event that something went wrong. All they knew was that something good was about to happen for the three of us. I told them not to worry. My boys were puzzled by my transformation, but they were both pleased with it. They knew that their momma was happy, and they liked the difference.

The Unsubstantiated Supervisor

With more determination than I had ever mustered before, I executed my God-given plans. I contacted a local moving company and finalized plans for the three of us to move on Saturday, June 12, 1976. It was emancipation day for the three of us. I instructed the moving company supervisor not to call my house to confirm the move because I did not want Vincent to know what was happening until we were gone, just in case he would try to prevent us from leaving. Although Vincent and I were both principals with the responsibility of running large schools, we handled our jobs differently. I stayed late almost every day to complete my paper work; Vincent was able to finish his and come home early.

Although the supervisor had assured me that he would not call to confirm the move, he called anyway. I was not at home, but Vincent was. At first, he was surprised that I would have the nerve to leave. Then he was angry.

Intimidation and Terrorization

My secretary took the call. She informed me that my husband was on the line and her troubled expression told me that something was wrong. When I picked up the receiver, Vincent yelled, "If you don't come home at once and explain to me what is going on, I am going around the corner to the basketball court to get the boys and do something terrible to them. You get here within the next ten minutes or else!"

Trembling, I put down the receiver. I was certain Vincent was capable of anything. After all, I had lived with this irrational maniac for nearly twenty years. Dexter and Lawrence loved basketball, and as a release from the stress that they endured in the house, I allowed them to play basketball on the court around the corner after school. They played with their friends until I came home from school to prepare dinner each evening. Vincent knew exactly where they were, and he knew I would come home immediately to protect them.

I left work immediately, giving some weak explanation to my office staff about why I had to hurry home. I hadn't confided in my co-workers about what was going on in my private world, though I am sure they suspected the worst. It took me only five to six minutes to get home, but by the time I pulled up, Vincent had already gone to the court and brought the boys home. When he saw me, Vincent told them to go back to the court and play, but they wanted to stay with me. I could see the terror in my sons' eyes as I drove up, but I assured them that everything was going to be just fine. Surprised by my unexpected poise, they seemed reassured.

An Astonishing Discovery

Vincent began to yell about the call from the moving company as soon as I arrived home. Naturally, he wanted to know what was going on. I looked Vincent square in the eye, calmly saying, "Yes, I am moving, and there is absolutely nothing that you can do to stop me!" He stared in disbelief. It was as if he were seeing me for the very first time.

Then, that man who had seemed so overwhelming and terrible for nearly twenty years did the very last thing that I would have expected him to do. He broke down and cried like a baby. In one moment, this imposing individual that had loomed larger than life for so long had become smaller than a child in my eyes. If the situation had not been so tragic, I would have burst out laughing.

Vincent was not done surprising me. He turned to the phone, dialed his mother in Philadelphia, and asked her to talk me into staying. While my mother-in-law was a woman whom I loved and respected, I had never revealed to her what was going on in my marriage. In my heart, I knew that she must have been aware of my situation. After all, she knew her son. When Vincent told her of my plans, his mother was so upset that she had a heart attack and had to be rushed to the hospital. I was sorry for what had happened to her, but my mind was made up. The lives of my children and my own were at stake. No matter what, Saturday would be moving day.

A Pitiful Sight

Vincent stayed home the Friday before our move. For my children and me, that Saturday was the happiest day of our lives. We packed our clothes and personal belongings, but we left him most of the furniture since Vincent had asked for it. When the movers arrived early that morning, we were ready to go. As they started up the stairs to load boxes, they were startled by the presence of a man lying in bed with the covers over his head. For the first time in my life, I was able to see Vincent for the pitiful excuse of a man that he had always been. He was a scared, small bully, and in that moment, I actually felt sorry for him. Still, I had to move on with my life. My sons and I had given him the best that we could through the years, and it wasn't enough. It was time to move on.

Free At Last

Our new apartment (which was only two blocks away) was empty except for our beds and the kitchen table with four chairs. It was all that we had to start over with, but we were oh-so happy. Now those years of torment were over. Finally my sons were at peace and were enjoying a period of contentment for the first time in their lives. I was now cheerful and in high spirits for the first time since I had gotten married nearly twenty years earlier. No longer were the three of us living in fear that we might say or do something that might "tick" off their dad and my husband. We could entertain in our own home. We could pull up the window shades and let in the sun light. Before, we had to keep our window shades pulled down tightly to keep both the sun and our neighbors out. The rooms were always dark and dreary to match Vincent's moods of depression. But now, that was all over. The first thing I remember doing when we moved into our new place was to paint our kitchen a bright yellow. To us, it represented sunshine and happiness. I also decorated the kitchen with bright, orange curtains to go along with the walls. Wow! It was bright! Company coming over needed to wear sunglasses to keep from being blinded by the glare of the bright light and color. To tell you the truth, the colors were almost comical and hilarious, but my sons and I thrived on those happy colors. We loved it! No longer were there needless restrictions. No more were there artificial barriers and lists of "what not to do." We could run and skip around the house like a bunch of weirdoes if we wanted to. Oh, my! It was wonderful! We could live and breathe just like regular people. It felt so good to our souls that it made us want to cry and laugh at the same time!

The Lord was our strength, and the three of us praised Him. We had come out of darkness into His marvelous light. Just like the final words in that great speech spoken by Dr. Martin Luther King, my sons and I were, "free at last, free at last, thank God almighty, free at last!"

And the Lord was with Jan...

the day I met husband number two

One thing I know, that, whereas I was blind, now I see.

John 9:25 (KJV)

Normalcy at Last

Now that my marriage to Vincent had ended, my boys and I were beginning to find true contentment. By now I had been an elementary school principal in the Gary, Indiana, school district for more than four years. I loved my job, and I also did volunteer work with the youth ministry in my home church. Both endeavors afforded me a sense of comfort and accomplishment. As a principal, however, I especially looked forward to the summer months. Most of the usual hassles and pressures of the school year were minimal or nonexistent, and there was time for me to formulate my plan for the upcoming school year.

Fleeting Thoughts

While driving home from school one afternoon, I felt a sense of peace and satisfaction. It was an unusual and fleeting feeling. Having lived so many years under stress and strain, I had almost forgotten what "normal" felt like. I wondered if I would ever meet the man of my dreams—my soul mate. But just as quickly as the thought came to me, I dismissed it and returned to the more mundane issues such as what I was going to prepare for dinner that evening.

City Beautification Campaign

Upon arriving home, I parked my car and walked toward my new residence—a modest, two-story duplex in a middle-income neighborhood within the city of Gary. Colleen, my next-door neighbor, was outside watering her lawn. As I approached her, she commented on what a difference a few budding plants were making in our neighborhood. She was right. It was incredible how beautiful our neighborhood was beginning to look.

It had been Colleen's idea that made me excited and committed to the beautification of our neighborhood. She had suggested that the two of us go to the neighbors on our block and suggest to them that we plant flowers in the front yards to beautify our community. It was true that none of us owned our own homes yet, and each month we collected rent receipts instead of earning equity on our mortgages. Even so, we still felt that we should take pride in our homes, and many of our neighbors agreed with us.

Responding to a Neighbor

As I approached Colleen that day after school, she greeted me with another bright idea. She suggested that the two of us help Lea, our neighbor, water her yard. Lea was a successful beautician who owned a thriving cosmetology business in the neighborhood, but she spent most of her time at her shop. Being a cooperative neighbor, Lea had hired a teenage boy to plant flowers in her front yard when Colleen and I approached her about neighborhood beautification, but she was rarely home to water her plants. I don't know what made Colleen think that I had time to water my neighbor's flowers. I agreed, but I first needed Lea's permission. Seeing her massive, white Cadillac Eldorado parked in front of her house, I felt that now would be a good time to speak to her. Colleen was determined and unrelenting and used to getting her way. So I headed down the block to present my plan to Lea.

A Chance Meeting

I was about to knock on Lea's door when I began to feel uneasy. What if she thought I was being pushy or insinuating that she should have been doing it herself? I still hadn't resolved my dilemma when I was faced with a handsome young man that had a striking resemblance to Lea. He greeted me with a warm smile as I explained why I was stopping by. The handsome stranger said that his mother was still at the shop, but he was almost certain she would be delighted for me to water the flowers for her.

With a charm that I had never before experienced, Harry introduced himself, and it wasn't long before he was showering me with questions. A bit flabbergasted, I told him my name and quickly excused myself. It was not my custom to talk with strangers, no matter how handsome or charming they might be. I returned to my duplex and found Colleen still watering her flowers. I told her that Lea was not at home and that I would return to talk with her later.

Twenty (or More) Questions

When I saw a second white Cadillac parked at Lea's, I returned to seek her permission firsthand. Once again, I was greeted by Harry, who once again informed me that Lea was not at home. But this time he was determined to pry a little conversation out of me. He mentioned that he was Lea's older son from Dallas and that he would be in Gary for only a few more days. With that out of the way, he immediately resumed his questions. I would later learn that after I left Lea's house the first time, he immediately phoned his younger sister Bonnie to inquire about me (she was a college student who was living at home and working in the salon during the summer months).

Bonnie told him that I was a principal, that I was divorced, that I lived alone with my two young sons, that no men visited regularly, that I was a Christian who enjoyed attending church, and that my sons and I were an extremely close-knit family. Harry had learned all of this about me before my return. He certainly hadn't wasted any time.

Answering the door a second time, he continued to pepper me with questions. Not only did I answer all of them, but I also volunteered information about myself that I had never shared before. His calm, reassuring manner began to tear down the walls of silence that I had erected years earlier as a defense mechanism.

Something New Happening

Never before had I met anyone with whom I could converse so effortlessly. He mentioned that he had just recently earned his master's degree and that he worked for the federal government in the Department of Agriculture. Harry was twenty-seven years old, which was ten years younger than I at the time. When he asked how old my first husband had been, I told him that Vincent had been five years older. Harry wanted to know if Vincent's age had meant that he was more mature. I had to think about that one, but I responded that his being older didn't mean that he was more mature. With confidence, Harry declared, "I rest my case. It is a proven fact that age is neither a plus nor a minus but only a number." And with that said, I never again made the difference in our ages a matter of consideration.

An Amazing Discovery

When I brought the conversation back to Lea's flowers, I thought that I heard him say that he could "hear" that they needed watering. It was at that moment that I noticed this young man was wearing sunglasses, even though we were inside the house. Wearing sunglasses inside a building in the 1970s meant that the person was usually visually impaired or even worse—blind. I examined Harry more closely, but I couldn't tell. His mannerisms did not give him away. Harry continued to talk with me, and having been starved for male conversation, I soaked up every morsel. Even though we were enjoying a pleasant conversation, I couldn't help but wonder if he really was blind.

I had to know, so finally I just came out and asked him.

"What did you mean when you said that you 'heard' that the flowers needed water?"

He corrected me, "I didn't say that, but sometimes blind people notice things that sighted people fail to see."

I was flabbergasted! "So you really are blind?"

"Yes," he laughed.

The tables had turned. I now had plenty of questions.

Questions, Questions, Questions...

Naturally, I didn't want to make Harry uncomfortable, so I chose my words carefully. I explained that I had never before known a blind person and asked if he would mind my asking him some basic questions.

He smiled graciously and told me to ask away. So I did.

Were you born blind?

How does it feel to not be able to see?

Are you totally blind or can you see a little bit?

What's the difference between total blindness and legal blindness?

Do the blind dream? If so, are their dreams in color or in black-and-white?

How do you eat?

Who dresses you?

How do you match your clothes? (I asked this because he was such a dapper dresser.)

How do you distinguish among the denominations of bills? Is there a different feel to a one dollar bill as opposed to a twenty dollar bill?

Has anyone ever cheated you and given you the wrong change?

How do you get around?

Do you have a guide dog? (I asked this because if he had a dog, I was out of there!)

Even though I asked a great many questions, he answered them all. But one answer impressed me the most.

I asked, "Harry, if God would grant to you your heart's greatest desire, what would you wish for?"

Harry responded, "If God granted me fifty wishes, my fifty-first desire would be for my sight. I 'see' more every day in my physical blindness and spiritual insight than most people see with their physical sight and spiritual blindness."

That impressed me greatly, and I *never* forgot that moment. It was a turning point in my life.

The time passed quickly. Before we knew it, the hour was late. Colleen had finished watering, and I had to get home. We exchanged telephone numbers (something else I had not done before). He said good night and promised to call me the next day.

That was Tuesday. Sure enough, the next day, he called me at school. I suppose he wanted to check to see if I really worked there as a principal. On Wednesday evening, he came over to my house with his sister Bonnie. I introduced Harry to my sons. They both liked him immediately, and he liked them as well. The three of them talked for hours, seemingly forgetting all about me. I didn't mind this, though, because their biological father rarely communicated with them.

An Invitation Declined

Later that evening, Harry invited me to accompany him to his grandmother's surprise birthday party the following month. He related that his grandmother was more like his real mom.

When Harry was born, he weighed only two-and-a-quarter pounds. He was placed in an incubator under intense light to keep him warm. It was never determined whether or not the lights from the incubator destroyed his retina and caused his blindness. Regardless, he had never been able to see. Because Lea, his mother, was only eighteen and unwed at the time of his birth, his grandparents brought him home from the hospital six months later and raised him as their own. To this day, Harry still calls his natural mother Lea, and his grandmother is "Momma."

"Momma" lived in Detroit, Michigan, and Harry had arranged for me to ride to the birthday party with his family. I hesitated to accept the invitation because I knew it would be impossible to make the round trip in one day. And staying overnight was out of the question for me. I refused his invitation, and Harry was very disappointed.

By now, Lea and Bonnie had seen how well Harry and I were hitting it off, and they were thrilled that the two of us had met. They both invited me to ride with them to the airport on Thursday when Harry would be catching his flight to Dallas. Harry and I both promised to keep in touch. We kept daily contact by phone, and a month later he returned to Gary for his grandmother's birthday party. Once again, Harry asked me to go with him to the party, and once again I refused. He did not press the issue but promised to go to church with me the following Sunday for communion. We made arrangements to meet at my house between five thirty and six in the evening in order to get to the seven o'clock service.

Sweet Anticipation Turned Sour

I didn't hear from Harry the entire weekend but found myself excited about going to church with him that Sunday. After all, my first husband had gone with me to church only twice in our nearly twenty years of marriage. Sunday came, and when 6:45 p.m. came and went, I realized that he was not coming. I wrote him off as a smooth operator and a liar. I went to church alone and took communion without him. When I still hadn't heard from him after returning home, I did my best to put him out of my mind.

The following morning, I saw Bonnie as I was preparing to drive to school. I told her that her brother was not a man of his word. "Harry had promised to go with me to church yesterday evening, and he didn't even have the decency to call and cancel. I am very disappointed in him."

Bonnie looked shocked! "You mean no one called you to tell you what happened?

"Called me to tell me what?"

Bonnie told me that her family had been involved in a terrible car accident on the way back home from Detroit. Two cars had been following each other when a car coming in the opposite direction lost control and hit broadside the car in which Harry had been traveling. Nearly all of the passengers in the car were able to anticipate the impact, so they were able to brace themselves for the collision.

Harry, on the other hand, was not able to brace himself for the impact. Being blind, he had no warning except for the screams of his family members. Everyone in the car escaped injury—except for him. He was rushed to the Paw Paw Hospital in Michigan and was kept there due to the seriousness of his injuries.

Jumping to False Conclusions

Suddenly, I understood why he had missed church that Sunday. I felt dreadful. I had thought the worst about him, and he could have been killed in the accident. I apologized to Bonnie, and she apologized for not telling me about the accident sooner. She also gave me the telephone number for his hospital room. I called and prayed with him as soon as I could regain my composure.

A few days later, Harry was released from the hospital. Due to the extent of his injuries, he was unable to return home to Dallas to his job with the federal government. He recuperated at Lea's, and we saw each other every day for the next six weeks. During that recuperation period, we grew closer.

Reflecting on that summer day, I realize that destiny had touched me. Colleen had been the matchmaker; I never would have been so bold without her persuasion. Lea, who had left her home and her husband to live in the duplex apartment for a short time, reconciled with her husband and returned home. Could it be that all of this happened because of God's providence? Did all of this happen because I was destined to meet Harry?

And the Lord was with Jan...

engagement number 2

Long Distance Romance

Forgetting those things which are behind, and reaching forth unto those things that are before.

Philippians 3:13 (KJV)

Getting to Know Him

Sometimes, I think that it's possible for something terrible to be a catalyst for a positive change. However, as strange as it might sound, Harry's automobile accident was perhaps one of the best things that could have happened to us. It changed the destiny for us both. Although his injuries were extensive, they were not life threatening. Nevertheless, both Lea and Bonnie had insisted that he remain with them in Gary so that they could nurse him back to health. During his weeks of recovery, I visited Harry regularly and got to know him better. I was fascinated by him. He looked just like a young Stevie Wonder in his late twenties, except that Harry did not sway his head back and forth as Stevie Wonder does. Harry had never attended a blind institution of learning; he had attended the public school in Gary for his entire youth. I couldn't imagine how he survived. As a former school teacher, I immediately sympathized with his classroom teachers. How had they been able to teach him? They weren't trained for such a specialty, and they didn't know Braille. Still, I thought it remarkable that Harry had managed to graduate from Emerson High School and go on to college.

Harry remained in Gary, and we began to see more of each other. I remember the first time he invited me out for dinner; it was to a restaurant called "The Big Wheel," which was located on the outskirts of the city. Naturally, I did the driving, but Harry was a perfect gentleman when we were ready to go. He walked me to the driver's side and held the door open for me as I slid under steering wheel. Then I started the car as he walked around to the passenger's side, opened the door, and got in—all without assistance. I had been married to a sighted husband for nearly twenty years, and he had never thought to open my door for me. I hardly knew whether I was more impressed by Harry's skill in maneuvering without sight or his social grace. When we arrived at the restaurant, he got out of the car first, walked around to the driver's side, opened my door for me, and helped me out of the car. *Now, what?* I thought to myself. But before I could get anxious, Harry took my hand, and just as if he could see where he was going, led us from the parking lot to the restaurant. Although I steered us, Harry was in command. Our movements together were so natural and comfortable that it seemed as if we had been doing this for ages.

Debunking Myths Regarding the Blind

Once we were seated, Harry asked for a Braille menu. I didn't know Braille menus even existed and was surprised when they brought one for him right away. As I glanced at my menu, I watched in fascination as his fingers glided across the raised bumps on the page of his menu. Sensing that I was paying attention to his reading, Harry told me that he was supposed to be reading with all of his ten fingers but that he had developed a technique that enabled him to read more quickly using his two index fingers. Once again, I was amazed. We took our time in comparing the two menus and pointing out the differences. When the waitress came, she asked me for my order and for Harry's, as well. He very politely reminded her, "I am blind, not deaf and dumb. I can speak and order for myself, if you don't mind."

The flabbergasted waitress was apologetic. "I am so sorry, sir. I did not mean to imply that… Oh, sir, I'm sorry!"

I smiled as I sympathized with the waitress. It was only a few weeks earlier that I had made the same assumptions regarding the blind. Harry went on to tell her that we all have handicaps—some are just more visible than others. We all laughed in agreement. Harry insisted that the waitress not concern herself about the error, and a tense moment was dissolved just like that. The evening was enchanting, and it was the first of many that Harry and I would enjoy together.

"Seeing" Eye to Eye

It wasn't long before I learned that Harry was the complete antithesis of Vincent. I felt completely at ease in his company. Because we had so much in common, we were never at a loss when it came to conversation. We could talk for hours about almost every topic under the sun. We both liked movies, music, books, museums, travel, sporting events, eating out at fabulous restaurants, and Bible study, especially. To me, our love for church and Jesus Christ was the icing on the cake.

Although Harry could not see me or rely upon my body language, he was more perceptive than any other male in my life had ever been with the exception of my father. Because Vincent never really talked to me, I had gotten out of the habit of looking people in the eyes when speaking to them. Shouting matches had been the norm for so long that looking away had become the normal thing to do. I wasn't even conscious of this habit until one day he said, "Look at me when you talk to me. Look me in my eyes."

I laughed inwardly, thinking, *Why should I look you in the eyes? You can't see if I'm looking at you or not.*

Immediately, as if he had read my mind, he replied, "I want to 'see' and hear what you have to say because what you say is important to me. I don't want to miss a word. So please look at me when you are speaking." From that moment on, I always spoke to him and everyone else while looking them straight in the eye.

Serious or Not?

The days passed quickly, and before long Harry had recovered sufficiently to return to work. In late September of 1977, he flew back to Dallas. Although we were thousands of miles apart, we communicated every day about the details of our lives. As time progressed, we grew closer and closer, despite our physical distance. We continued our relationship this way for two years with no ill effects—outside of our enormous telephone bills. It became obvious to us, my sons, and our family and friends that things between Harry and me were quite serious. Harry had begun dropping hints about a short engagement period and a June or July wedding in 1978. I needed to be absolutely sure, however, that I wasn't about to make another terrible mistake.

Marriage has always been a very serious matter to God. He has plenty to say about it in His Word, and this time I wanted to do things God's way. Trying to handle things my way had been completely disastrous as my time with Vincent had illustrated. I needed to be absolutely certain that Harry was the man for me. But how could I gauge such a thing? Feelings are too fickle and fleeting to be trusted. Besides myself, I had my two sons to consider in the matter. What did they want? It was clear to me that they had grown to love and respect Harry, but how would they feel about moving from Indiana to Texas? Would they want to change schools and move a thousand miles away from their closest friends? Dexter was entering his senior year of high school at Bishop Noll. How would he feel about leaving all that was familiar to him when he perhaps needed it the most? I felt as though Dexter needed to stay for at least another year. Both Dexter and Lawrence had already sacrificed far too much in their young lives.

Pondering

What would Harry say to the request that we delay our wedding plans until Dexter graduated from high school? In my way of thinking, if Harry was agreeable to my request to wait until after Dexter's graduation to marry, then that would be a clear sign. If Harry appeared angry or unhappy, then I would know in my heart that he was not the man for me.

Harry wholeheartedly agreed that we should wait a year to allow Dexter to graduate with his classmates at Bishop Noll. He also encouraged Dexter to apply to a college in Texas where he could be close to us after the move. Dexter had his heart set on attending Indiana State University in Terre Haute. Although Harry and I were disappointed with Dexter's decision, we told him that we would honor our agreement to pay his tuition and housing as long as he kept up his grades and did not transfer. It seemed like a win-win situation for all of us.

Some Questions Answered, but Still Uncertain

I still felt as though I needed greater assurance that Harry was the one that God wanted me to marry. Harry must have sensed my reluctance and uncertainty because he proposed a spiritual solution to my dilemma.

Harry suggested that the two of us pray and fast for five straight days in order to seek spiritual guidance. We both needed to hear from the Lord regarding our future together, so I agreed. I had heard sermons about fasting and had read about it in Scripture. I knew that Jesus had fasted and prayed for forty days and nights before selecting His twelve disciples.

Fasting was very difficult for me; those five days seemed like an eternity. I began to obsess over food. Though I thought about different delicacies, I didn't succumb to the temptation to break my fast. When I got desperate enough to sneak a bite of something, I would pray hard, and soon the hunger sensations subsided. When the five days were finally over, I did not know how to come off of a fast. So I ate what I had been craving during those five long days—a Philly cheese-steak sandwich. When I bit into that Italian roll stuffed full of juicy beef and grilled onions and peppers, I thought it was heavenly—that is until I spent the next day or two as sick as a dog.

Spiritual Confirmation and Contentment

More important than the end of the fast was that God had spoken to both Harry and me about our relationship. We were meant to be together, and I now felt peaceful and content. Harry proposed to me at the Magic Pan Restaurant in Chicago. The waiter brought dessert on a silver tray with a small black box containing my engagement ring. It was a magical moment that I will never forget.

The Reactions of Family and Friends

Although Harry and I were sure about each other, some of my close friends and relatives were afraid that I was biting off more than I could chew. Many of them suggested that it would not be in my best interests to get involved with an individual who was visually challenged. They felt that I had not adequately assessed the ramifications, and they wanted to be sure that I knew what life would be like living with a blind husband.

This time, I listened carefully to whatever my friends and relatives had to say because I knew they loved me and wanted the best for me. My answer was always the same, though. Yes, I knew what I was in for, and I was prepared to do whatever was needed. I assured them that I had prayed about my decision and that there was nothing to worry about. Most were reassured by my response, but some were very dubious about Harry and lamented that I was giving up a bright future. I knew that I could never convince everyone to agree with me, but I still loved them for caring enough to share their concerns.

Wedding plans were the next big, welcome challenge.

And the Lord was with Jan...

married for love: one in college and one in diapers

Love beareth all things, believes all things, hopes all things, endures all things.

1 Corinthians 13:7 (KJV)

The Commitment to Adopt is Serious Business

During my first marriage, I had never thought about adopting a child. Why should I have? After all, I had been blessed to give birth to two healthy, bouncing baby boys exactly three years and one month apart.

Boys were always my favorite, and God had given me exactly what I had prayed for. My family size was perfect—mother, father, plus two —we four, and no more.

Adoption Wasn't a Consideration...at First

However, I met Harry, and the topic of adoption came up. Wanting to be completely open and honest, I informed Harry from the very beginning that I was unable to give him a child naturally because I had experienced medical problems sixteen years earlier during my last pregnancy. The baby's delivery had been unusually difficult and full of medical complications. The doctors feared for the lives of both my baby and me. Thank God that both of us survived; however, the doctors informed me I would not be able to have additional children. It was then that I learned that Harry had never wanted to father a child of his own. He said that he had always wanted to adopt because he did not want to increase the chances of producing a blind child. Although there was no other blind person in his family background that he knew of, he would not have wanted his own biological son or daughter to have to experience blindness. Harry had made tremendous adjustment to his world of darkness. It was also true that his inability to see had never been detrimental to his academic progress or social development, but he did not want that type of emotional challenge for his child—especially a daughter. Harry had always felt he was more of an exception to the rule than the norm. He had many friends who had not made the adjustments and were negatively affected by their visual handicap all of their lives.

After Harry and I were married, we once again discussed the subject of adoption along with our sons. We decided together that we would adopt a baby girl. Dexter and Lawrence had always wanted a little sister. My hysterectomy had slashed all hopes of my ever having a baby sister for the boys, but now our dreams were being revived. The four of us were excited thinking about "the pitter-patter of little feet" one day running around our home.

The Process of Adoption Is Arduous

Neither Harry nor I knew anything about the adoption process. We had often heard encouragement to adopt over the media. It all sounded so easy, so wonderful, and so philanthropic; however, we had been misled. Adoption is no cake walk. It is hard work. There is no other word to describe it. The adoption process is long, difficult, and expensive. Now that we had made the decision to adopt a baby, the first thing we needed to do was contact a local adoption agency and make the initial inquiry. We made the contact, but once the agency realized Harry was blind and I was over forty with two natural biological sons of my own, the agency refused to consider us as potential adoptive parents. Many on the adoption panel felt Harry and I would not be suitable parents because he was "visually challenged" and I was too old to start parenting again. And yet we knew their judgment was flawed. We personally knew several couples who were successfully raising their own children, yet both parents were totally blind or visually impaired. I was born when my mother was thirty-three and my dad was forty-six, and they made outstanding parents. What was this agency talking about? This was ridiculous! However, we went from one agency to another, only to hear the same negative rebuffs. Now, most married couples might have become discouraged or even given up, but not us. Harry and I were resolute in our determination to get our child as an infant so that together we could make the greatest impact upon that young life. What did we do? We prayed and sought the counsel of those who had previously gone through the rigid adoption process.

Difficulty Finding a Receptive Agency

Finally, without any success with the other numerous agencies, we were told to contact the Lutheran Adoption Agency in Dallas. From the very beginning, there was a vast contrast. The reception was positive and reassuring with our initial contact. A social worker was selected, and she made numerous visitations to our home. She asked extensive questions about our family backgrounds, our childhood experiences, and our present circumstances. Not only did she interview Harry and me together, but she also interviewed us both separately. To me, that was particularly hilarious because Harry and I had always disagreed about how exactly we met, and we kidded each other about our conflicting memories of how it happened. When we spoke separately to the counselor, our recollections were so radically different that it almost cast a shadow of doubt on our truthfulness. Harry and I laughed about it, but unfortunately, it was not funny to our social worker who did not have a sense of humor.

The entire adoptive process was put on hold until we could sort out the details and agree on how we really met. (Of course, my version was correct). I believe that we may have unwittingly put our chances for adoption in jeopardy without realizing it, but our prayers prevailed, and the process continued without further interruption. We had to undergo full medical examinations at our own expense. We also had to give the adoption agency's medical advisor a report covering our own and our family's health history. The home study assessment was demanding and even somewhat intrusive. Everything about us was explored in depth. Understandably, adoption is for life, and the agency had to make sure we were right for the role we both were about to undertake.

Lawrence, who was by now a junior in high school, was interviewed, also. The agency placed a great deal of credence in his comments and emotional reactions to the baby. If he, at age sixteen, had given even the slightest indication that he was not in favor of having a baby sister the process would have been over. Dexter was not interviewed or considered in the adoption process because he was away at college in Indiana. He was, however, disappointed that his enthusiastic views had not been considered as part of the record. The entire grueling adoption assessment and approval process took about eight months. Once we were approved, we had to endure the tedious process of being matched with a suitable child. Brandi, our baby girl, was born September 19, 1980, but we didn't receive our bundle of joy until ten days later. It was a rainy Monday, September 29 that we went to the agency to hold our baby girl for the first time. Oh, how beautiful she was! I can't express the joy we felt over the blessing that only God could have bestowed on our family. Harry and I adopted our baby daughter when she was only ten days old and we had been married for one year. Both of our boys adored their new baby sister.

My Sanity and Judgment are Seriously Questioned

Starting over again from scratch with diapers, baby, and the whole nine yards in my forties was a sheer joy for me. However, many of my friends thought I had lost my ever-loving mind. They thought that I either was an angel in disguise or had gone through the change of life that had melted my brain, rendering me insane. After all, what was I thinking? Wasn't raising your children to become adults exactly the goal every clear-thinking parent wished for? Didn't parents want to be free once again to do what they wanted to do with their lives? None of my friends could understand why I would subject myself to child rearing all over again with an ambitious husband who had grand ideas but needed my help to execute them. My friends were upset with me, but I totally disagreed with them. Because of my love for my sons, my new baby, and Harry, and my need to please him and perform as the perfect wife and mother, I gladly gave it all I had. Yes, there were difficulties, stresses, and strains, but I was up to the challenge. I was happy, and I was fulfilled.

The Idea of Adoption Originated with God

Adopting my baby daughter was the best thing that came out of my marriage to Harry. I am so thankful that the Lord blessed me with her. Brandi is as much my child as her two brothers. The only difference is that I did not give physical birth to her. However, I have gone through every other emotional, mental, psychological, and spiritual emotion that I have with my two natural off-springs. For me, adoption was just as binding and bonding.

I have often thanked Brandi's biological mother for delivering rather than destroying a baby she could not keep and care for. God used her physical body to conceive and carry the child I couldn't have after my hysterectomy. In God's magnificent and matchless sovereignty, He connected two women who never had the opportunity to meet face to face but who will interact together for the rest of their lives by way of a precious baby named Brandi. To this unknown woman, I will be eternally grateful.

But the Lord was with Jan...

God has a great sense of humor

"He that sitteth in the heavens shall laugh."
(Psalm 4:2, KJV)

Conflicting Wills

Does God have a will for every life? Yes, I believe God has a plan for every believer's life—especially the life of a pastor's wife, but I never wanted to be one. To be a first-lady would have been my worst nightmare.

My sister Ada and I, as youngsters, would sit in the church pews and ignore the preachers on the rostrum, instead focusing our gaze on the wives of those "blessed" men. Even then, we saw something sad and restrained in their eyes. To Ada and me, preachers' wives seemed lonely because most of the other female church members ignored them or interacted with them very little.

No one ever talked to us about their roles, but one thing was for sure; we knew we didn't want to be one of them. As a matter of fact, we were definitely determined *not* to marry a preacher man.

God Laughs

Believe it or not, our God has a real sense of humor. Yes, He really does. How do I know? I know because both my sister and I grew up and married men who were called into the ministry as preachers and later pastors.

Never say what you will or will not do—because you may end up doing that very thing. It was the will of God that both of us become "first ladies."

My husband actively sought to be considered as a viable candidate for pastor at many churches—one being Sweet Water Baptist Church (SWBC), in Round Rock, Texas. I was interviewed numerous times as well, and it was at SWBC that I was asked the most probing questions.

I was quizzed about my Bible knowledge and my belief in Jesus Christ. They even presented some hypothetical situations to see how I would react under trying conditions. Apparently, the search committee had been impressed with Harry, and I must have given satisfactory answers as well because they stepped out of the room, discussed both of us, and after a short period of time, re-entered smiling.

A few days later, my husband received a phone call and then a letter requesting him to preach on a designated date and time. He was informed that the congregation would vote to determine whether he would be their next pastor.

SWBC was one of the friendliest and most professional of all the churches my husband had been privileged to be a candidate. The Pulpit Committee chairperson was a spirit-filled man who made sure that everything was done decently and in order. I was excited for my husband at the prospect of his being chosen pastor. It took a spiritually mature flock to want a blind leader—physically blind but certainly not spiritually blind.

I had one concern, however, and to me, it was a serious concern. The church had a long list of prior pastors. I knew that most churches keep their pastors for many years. Some pastors even stay until the Lord calls them home in death. Both of my former pastors had led their flocks for over forty years.

So when I read the history of SWBC and realized that the church had been in existence since 1895 and had already had sixteen pastors, I was very concerned. If you divided the number of pastors by the date the church originated, the average pulpit stay of each pastor was about five years. That's generally the tenure of a local superintendent for most school boards—but not for pastors of God's churches. Most of them serve for thirty, forty, or fifty years or more or until they pass away.

I discussed my concern with my husband and suggested that maybe he should reconsider his acceptance and continue looking. To me, this was an indication that something was not right about this church. But, of course, he disagreed and thought I was being silly and irrational. The next Sunday in November of 1988, he preached, the congregation voted, and he was the new pastor of Sweet Water Baptist.

Although I was nervous and had my doubts about the large number of previous pastors, I put my fears behind me and began to walk by faith in a way I had never walked before.

I was saved—I knew the Lord. I trusted Him for most things, but the moment I became "First Lady" of the church, I began to pray and read my Bible as if my life depended on it...And my life *did* depend on it!

And the Lord was with Jan...

a strange
first lady

"But ye are a chosen generation, a royal priest-hood, a holy nation, a peculiar people" (1 Peter 2:9, KJV).

A Call to the Ministry

Having been married for almost ten years, Harry and I had spent many years applying to churches, going through the interview process, and preaching trial sermons only to repeatedly endure the pain of rejection from people unwilling to accept a blind man as their spiritual leader. I had nearly given up hope of Harry's ever achieving his goal, but his faith was steadfast. Finally, the cycle of raised hopes and crushing rejection was over. We were finally going to be the first family of a wonderful church.

We immediately made plans for the move from Dallas to Round Rock, which was a flourishing community near Austin. We listed our home, and Harry turned in his resignation from the Department of Agriculture. I stayed behind in Dallas in order to finish the school year, to job search, and to close on the sale of our home. Everything went as planned, and God was with us every step of the way.

Jan Newell-Byrd

Adjusting to a New Church Family and Roles in Ministry

Those early years of working together in the ministry were a heavenly time for me. The members of Sweet Water Baptist Church were loving and generous to their new Pastor and First Lady. At that time, the church had fewer than seventy-five members. For whatever reason, Harry's blindness was not an issue for the congregation, and although his salary was significantly less than what he had earned with the government, the church made up the difference in other ways. They did whatever they could to ensure that our needs were met, and both of us were satisfied with our blessings from the Lord.

Although the congregation was small, its members were extremely progressive and tech-savvy. Many of the members worked at IBM or Dell, which was an added blessing—Harry's administrative assistant and deacons researched and acquired equipment that enabled the pastor to transcribe his sermons in Braille onto his own, special computer. He would no longer need to type his lessons manually. Only God could have done something so wonderful for us.

Preaching to the People

Shortly after Pastor Harry's installation service, he was able to fully share his spiritual gifts of administration, preaching, and teaching with the congregation. I was extremely proud of my husband (if a bit protective, at times), and I believed that Harry had a pastor's heart and love for the people of God. We were both so grateful to God for honoring our desire to serve a church of such wonderful people. I continued to research his sermons for him because there were very few commentaries available in Braille. In fact, when Harry had announced his desire to preach years earlier, I had arranged for a Matthew-Henry commentary to be sent to New York and transcribed into Braille for him. The cost of that one book was over two thousand dollars, and that was in 1983. It was comprised of 225 Braille volumes and occupied six shelves in the library. There was absolutely no way that we could have afforded to transcribe additional commentaries into Braille. Even if we could have, we would never have had enough room to store such a massive collection. Therefore, it was up to me to provide him with what he needed in order to successfully minister.

As I researched commentaries and scripture, I gave him the information on tape each night. Harry listened to it and then transcribed my notes into Braille, preparing his messages and preaching his sermons with their emphasis on the Word of God. We were quite the team. We worked, studied, prayed, and managed the ministry all together—though I was always in the background. Only Harry's administrative assistant, the chairman, and other leaders in the church knew exactly what my role was.

Harry preached on Sunday mornings and evenings and taught the Bible lessons on Wednesday evenings. His exegesis of Scripture led the congregation to grow in size and spiritual insight. By 1992, we had outgrown our current building, and we worried that the Round Rock fire marshal would eventually cite us for being over capacity. It was a wonderful problem to have, but it meant that we would need to purchase a new building or construct a new church. Soon, Sweet Water Baptist Church and its pastor were the talk of the community—even into Austin. Harry was overjoyed by the attention, and I was proud of my husband.

Learning to Discover and Discern

Though I had been active in church affairs nearly my entire life, it was only after serving as First Lady that I began to recognize the two types of people in a church—the real and the false, the saved and the lost, the possessors of Christ and the spiritually pretentious, "what's-in-it-for-me" type of folks. I also soon realized that a church's First Lady needed to be smart and attractive, and she had to have enough vigor to keep the church's "husband snatchers" at bay. One would be amazed at the bold overtures that so-called "church women" would make toward their pastor. Harry may have been physically blind, but it was I who was blind in other ways. Initially, the actions of a few of the women left me feeling naïve and pitifully immature, but I fast became an expert at the cat-and-mouse games that some of these women played.

The "fairer" sex surely has some unfair ways of attracting men—especially those with wives. It didn't take a rocket scientist to realize that a few such women wanted my husband for themselves. While most were discrete, a few were forthright with their intentions. They positioned themselves in the Pastor's Aide Circle or whichever ministry they could join that would give them an excuse to be close to him. There were also those who would run up to the pastor after service, trying to be ever-so-helpful (and a bit too helpful, if you ask me). They certainly got on my nerves, and at times it was difficult to conceal my annoyance. If they had only done for their own husbands at home what they were trying to do for their pastor in church, I am certain they would have been much happier. I do believe that a few of these women felt that they could do a much better job of being me than I could. Despite his blindness, Harry was quite handsome and extremely personable. Women found that winning combination of character and charisma irresistible. He was the perfect target for the desires of weak, lonely women—both single and married.

But having a blind husband was not easy. I had to do far more than the wife of a sighted man, and those women weren't aware of just how difficult my job was. Harry could never pick out his own clothing, a simple but important, job. Naturally that task fell to me. I loved him, and to me, it was just another wifely duty. When it came to my husband, my children, and my household, I wanted to be the virtuous woman found in Scripture (Proverbs 31). Most of the congregation appreciated my efforts in keeping their pastor appropriately-attired. No matter how hard I tried, though, there were always a few who were never satisfied with what I selected for him. If I dressed him in white shirts, they felt that he should wear colored shirts. Some felt I dressed him too conservatively—like an old man. Others felt that I dressed him too "hip." I knew that I could not please everyone, so I didn't let it bother me too much. After all, I had the final say.

Making Many Mistakes

Throughout this time of rapid growth in the church, Harry and I continued to attend seminary. I was seemingly the only First Lady who did not remain in the background of her husband's ministries and assume a subordinate role. Although Harry was serving full-time as pastor, I taught eighth grade in the Round Rock school system by day and attended seminary with him in the evenings. Some thought my ambitions strange, but I loved my husband, the church members, and the rigors of biblical scholarship.

I wanted to assist Harry in pursuing his doctoral degree in biblical studies, and I wanted to pursue my degree as well. But Harry had convinced me that a pastor's wife would be undermining her husband's position by pursuing the same degree. He also stressed that the church was only obligated to pay for his degree since he was the Pastor. My degree would have to be budgeted from our family income. I accepted his judgment for two reasons. First, I loved him, and second, I felt that he truly had my best interests at heart. After all, we were a team, and both of us were God's servants. Right?

But, I still felt that I needed that piece of paper. I could hear my dad's voice and feel his hand on my shoulder, urging me to be wise and to do what my heart and mind were telling me to do. Yes, hind sight is twenty/twenty.

So when Harry returned to seminary after accepting his call to the ministry, I was right there supporting him. Harry enrolled as a graduate student, but I entered as an auditor of the same classes. Though I was not officially enrolled as a student and did not pay for the classes, I completed every assignment that the professors gave. In fact, I did more than Harry and many of the other students as I completed all the assignments, read all the textbooks, researched papers, and took all the tests for my husband as well as for myself. I did so because none of the material was available in Braille. Harry had tried to take his own notes in class, but the clanking noises of the Braille writer drowned out the lectures. So Harry (and especially his classmates) embraced the idea of my sitting in class and taking his notes for him. Eventually, we discontinued face-to-face classes and worked toward his degree via correspondence, a change which enabled us to progress at a much faster pace.

Still, I could hear my father's words echoing, "Get that piece of paper… You need that diploma!" I didn't heed my father's warning. Harry was my husband. What was his was mine… wasn't it? And that decision not to pursue my degree was perhaps the one that I have regretted most over the years.

My Compassionate and Caring
Sisters-in-Christ

It took Harry nearly ten years to complete it, but he earned his doctoral degree in divinity in 1994. The precious sisters of the church bestowed me with an honorary doctorate degree. I was deeply honored. I knew that it was their way of recognizing what I had done for their pastor. That gesture of love and compassion touched my heart and endeared them to me in a way they will never know. The honorary degree plaque hangs on my wall to this very day.

My Expanded Role as First Lady

As Harry's counseling load increased, so did rumors of his inappropriate behavior toward women of the church. As a result, Harry begged me to retire from teaching in the public school system and come work full-time in the ministry. He said it would not only lighten my work load, but we could work together and be with one another all day. Like a dummy, I agreed. The idea was presented to the church membership, and they readily agreed with the plan. The church staff warmly welcomed me, also. It had not occurred to me, however, that perhaps Harry was trying to pull me into the picture in order to make him appear less guilty of the rumors that were continuing to circulate.

At the end of the school year, I did retire from the public school system and started working full time at the church. My ministry responsibilities at Sweet

Water were numerous. I served as Christian Education Director, Sunday School Teacher, Youth Director for students ages five through eighteen, Ministers' Wives and Deaconess Ministry Leader, Vacation Bible School Coordinator, biblical researcher and writer, and, of course, First Lady of a growing church. My work load was enough to choke a horse, to say the least. In addition to my responsibilities at church, I still had to maintain my home. Brandy was a growing teen, and both my eighty-eight-year-old mother and Harry's eighty-seven-year-old grandmother were living with us. They required my attention and care. I loved them, but my plate was full.

And the Lord was with Jan...

an ugly
church fight

Agree with thine adversary quickly, whiles thou
art in the way with him; lest at any time the
adversary deliver thee to the judge, and the
judge deliver thee to the officer, and thou be
cast into prison.

Matthew 5:25 (KJV)

By 1995, the church membership had begun to drop
off significantly as rumors of the pastor's inappropriate behavior increased. The building fund was in jeopardy and the spiritual atmosphere of the church continued to deteriorate. Harry's ability to preach and
teach had been adversely impacted by his refusal to
study and take his ministry seriously. Now there was
a growing discontent in some of the prominent leaders of the church, and they wanted to remove him as
pastor. The few deacons who still felt favorably toward
Harry met and tried to reason with him. But instead of
Harry's humbling himself and listening to his leaders,
he became belligerent and refused to cooperate. After
that unsuccessful meeting, the growing number of discontented members met secretly to make plans to take
Harry to court and legally dismiss him as pastor.

Here Comes the Judge

The judge was reluctant to rule in a spiritual matter. Instead, he recommended that the complaint be taken back to the congregation. A church-wide vote would be held, under the supervision of the district church moderator and a representative from the police force. The meeting was set for Tuesday, March 6, 1996, at 7:00 p.m. and letters were sent to all active members.

Ordinarily, only a few people attended a Tuesday evening business meeting, but this was no ordinary meeting. This was sure to be a spectacle. Even though it was raining "cats and dogs" and flash flood warnings had been issued, people came out in droves. Even the "CME' members (those who usually only show up for Christmas, Mother's Day, and Easter services) made it their business to come out that particular evening. It was time to vote to keep the pastor or throw him out, and no one was going to miss this juicy event—no matter what the weather.

The church had been thrown into the midst of a spiritual storm. Rumors of Harry's inappropriate behavior with certain females of the congregation were wide spread. Harry had received phone calls from people keeping up with the scandal from Austin, Dallas, Houston, and even as far away as California and Harlem, New York. By now, members had divided themselves into two distinct factions: those solidly behind their pastor and those who wanted to "throw the rascal out."

A few hours before the business meeting that evening, Harry had pulled me aside at home to warn me that there might be a woman or two who could possibly come forward and say that he had behaved inappropriately with them, but he said that I should dismiss their allegations because they were not true. He said that they were interested in him romantically, but when he refused their advances, they became vindictive and swore to get even. He also told me that he loved me and that these women just wanted to break up our marriage. He pleaded with me not to let that happen.

"Dressed to Kill"

The time of the meeting arrived. As we entered and were ushered to our reserved seats in the standing-room-only sanctuary, a hush fell over the entire congregation. I could feel their eyes looking us over. I had carefully picked out navy and white outfits for my entire family and made sure we all looked sharp. I sat looking stylish and polished on the outside, but broken and devastated on the inside. I wondered how long I would be able to sit quietly and listen as numerous women came forth to accuse my husband of infidelity—so many women that I finally lost count. Nevertheless, I sat looking calm and collected alongside my daughter, my mother, and "Big Momma," my husband's grandmother. It was one of the most horrifying experiences of my entire life. I just wanted to run. I wanted to scream. I wanted the floor to open up and swallow me alive, but of course it didn't. I just sat and listened and listened and … It was like a horrible nightmare that wouldn't end, and no matter how hard I tried to shake myself, I couldn't wake up. Surely, this wasn't happening for real. It couldn't be! As painful as the ordeal was for me, it was just as damaging and terrible for my teenage daughter, Brandi, and our elderly moms, who had to sit and hear accusations and incriminations hurled against their father, grandson, and son-in-law. On the other hand, being a woman of God proved to be a wonderful blessing. As I sat, I prayed for strength to endure this torture, and slowly the peace of God began to sweep all over me. I could feel the Lord holding me fast in the palm of His hand, and I knew we would survive.

Takes Two to Tango

The business meeting continued well into the night. I thought it would never end. As woman after woman came forward to voice complaints, I wondered why at least one of them had not come to me earlier about Harry's advancements. After all, many of these same women had visited with me in my home and had acted like they were my friends or at least my sisters-in-Christ. So if Harry had really been unfaithful (and I was not absolutely convinced that he had), they certainly must have been willing participants. It couldn't have been all one-sided. After all, Harry couldn't "run after them" or drive them to a secluded spot, because he was blind. How much could a blind man do without a lot of cooperation on the other person's part?

Finally, the last accuser came forward, and it was time to make a decision. But just before the votes were to be cast, the court-appointed moderator asked me to step forward and speak. I was keenly aware that everything hinged on what I, Harry's wife and the First Lady of the church, would have to say. However, I had not prepared a speech, even though Harry had said I might be called. And any way, whatever I might have written in preparation couldn't possibly have been a valid response to what I had heard because it would have been based upon what Harry had told me. I determined that I would just let the Lord speak through me. As I stepped up to the microphone, everyone held their breath. I could sense the tension in the air. *Would she stand by her man or would she throw him to the wolves?*

Standing Tall and Taking a Stand

As I looked over the congregation, I felt strangely at ease. The Holy Spirit was at work in me. I could plainly see that there were two distinct sets of people waiting to vote: those who would vote in favor of Pastor and me, and the others who would vote to cast us out. It was clearly discernable on their faces, even before I spoke. The only question was which group was larger.

I began to speak, but I don't remember exactly what I said. I do remember, however, reviewing the history of all the good things Harry had done for the church from 1989 to the present time. I reminisced about how far we had come through Pastor's biblical teaching and preaching and how we had all grown spiritually. I then told the congregation that I didn't believe what I had heard from the women and gave my reasons why. I ended by saying I loved my husband and I was standing by him. Then I sat down. With those brief remarks, some were shocked and disappointed; others were pleased, but they all gave me a thunderous applause.

After I spoke, the church voted, and Harry won. He would remain the pastor.

And the Lord was with Jan...

PART THREE:
deception, betrayal, and rejection

the storm is passing over

And there arose a great storm of wind, and the
waves beat into the ship, so that it was now full;
And He said unto the sea, "Peace, be still."

Mark 4:37, 39 (KJV)

Weathering Storms of Turbulence and Confusion

After Harry won the church vote and was declared to
still be the pastor, many who were against Harry were
visibly upset. The results were hotly contested. The
moderator confirmed, however, that the majority had
voted to keep their pastor, and the vote was valid and
final. A few of the deacons, however, decided to take
matters into their own hands. Sometime later they
changed the locks on the doors of the church and locked
the pastor out. They even tried to intimidate Harry
and threatened him, telling him not to return to the
pulpit or he might be harmed. The chief of police had
to be called, and a few Sunday morning services were
interrupted due to the actions of the more disgruntled
church officers. Pastor's opponents had anointed themselves as leaders of the "real" church.

During its heyday from 1989 to 1994, Sweet Water Baptist had blossomed from seventy-five to over one thousand members. Weekly attendance had grown so large that there was a need for two Sunday worship services. A building plan had been instituted for a new church, and money had begun pouring in. But between the years of 1996 and 1999, the church went through two divisive fights, and although Pastor and Sweet Water Baptist Church had won the battles, they lost the war. Though Sweet Water still enjoyed Pastor's biblical teaching and sermons, more than half of the membership had left to join other churches. A few stopped going to church all together because they had found it difficult or downright impossible to worship in an atmosphere that had become much more circus-like than spiritual.

The Domino Effect

Soon, there was no longer a need for the building program. The construction plans were scrapped, and building funds were used to defray court fees. Meanwhile, the meager church offerings could no longer cover all of the expenses and staff salaries. Loyal members voted to continue Pastor's salary at his former rate, but many other full-time church staff members were either released or cut from full time to part time. My position was cut out completely, and I was forced to return to teaching school. However, I continued to offer my services to the church on a volunteer basis since I was the pastor's wife. Most congregations considered the pastor and his wife as a package deal, anyway. I'm sure that the congregation knew that I would never stop researching and writing the biblical studies for Pastor's sermons.

Troubles with a Capital "T"

Together Harry and I made a great team. I had stood up for him when it would have been far easier for me to walk out on him, but Harry still didn't seem appreciative. And although he had asked me to retire from my public school teaching position and work at the church, it was never clear to me whether Pastor (as I had come to call him) had hired me to relieve me from the double duty of working at school and volunteering many hours at church, or whether he wanted me at the church to deflect the persistent rumors within the community regarding inappropriate behavior between him and members of the opposite sex. Harry was a complex man and was not above taking risks. On the other hand, he was calculating and seldom did anything without weighing the pros and cons of his actions.

As wonderful and as beautiful the first years had been, the last five or six years at Sweet Water Baptist turned out to be the most difficult and stressful years of my life.

Double for My Trouble

Working without a salary for the church did not hurt my pride or our finances. I was re-hired at Harris Elementary School by my former principal, Mildred Sanders, who welcomed me as a fifth grade teacher. My full time teaching salary was actually double what I had been making at the church, so losing my position at the church and returning to the school system was advantageous for me, my husband, and the church. God is always good.

Even though Pastor and I had weathered the storm in some respects, the church fights had broken my heart. Though I did not let it show, I was deeply wounded by what we had allowed others to do to us. Harry and I should have known better. The sense of embarrassment and defeat was almost more than I could bear, and I spent too many nights in tears during those dreadful years.

Needless to say, Harry and I continued to be the talk of the church community, but something hurt me even more deeply than the gossip. It was the lack of friendship or empathy from First Ladies of other churches in the area. All of them knew me, and some personally, yet not one called or wrote me to express concerns or support or even to offer a prayer, despite the fact that we were all members of a group comprised of pastor's wives. I simply could not understand their lack of compassion.

During this time of turbulence, I continued full responsibility for the care of my husband and served as primary caregiver for our two elderly parents who lived with us. My mother had lived with Harry and me for many years, and she was a constant delight in our home. Still, my concern for her steadily increased as she grew older and her health declined. It was a tremendous blow to our family when she passed away just four months short of her ninetieth birthday. I had taken her to the doctor earlier that week for her three month check-up, and she had been given a clean bill of health, which made her death all the more devastating. For me, it was doubly dark and sad. Oh, how I missed my mother! Her death took more out of me than I could have imagined.

Home Alone, At Last

A few weeks before my mother passed away, Harry's grandmother decided she was going to return to Gary and live with her elder daughter, Harry's mother. Brandi, our daughter, was now away at college. Now I was no longer the primary caregiver for my elderly family members, and I had more time for myself. Harry and I were now empty nesters. We were now able to spend more time together and enjoy one another, but Pastor was seldom home. He was spending the majority of his time counseling at the church or traveling with speaking engagements. Internally, I was still stressed over the church and its problems, but I remembered one of my favorite Bible verses: "And this too shall pass." It reminded me of the importance of understanding that events in life do not come to stay. Even with the comfort of that particular piece of Scripture, I realized that I had come to the end of another road in my life, and it was now time for me to move along.

Reaching a Historic Milestone

Life moves on. Harry and I had been Pastor and First Lady of Sweet Water Baptist Church now for more than twelve years. We had weathered the storms (a publicly humiliating court ruling and two church schisms) and had set a record by serving longer than any other First Couple in the ninety-eight year history of the church. The remaining members were loyal and loved Harry. They were willing to follow his lead, and the church was finally beginning to settle into a spiritually harmonious routine. The turbulent days appeared to be behind us. It was a brand new year, and I felt refreshed. When April rolled around, I began planning for Vacation Bible School 2000. Oh, how I loved it! I had prayed that God would help me to make this year's the biggest and best program that our church had ever experienced. I believed that God was about to do something great in my life through this undertaking.

And the Lord was with Jan...

facing the pain of infidelity

Thou shalt not commit adultery.

Exodus 20:14 (KJV)

It is devastating to learn that someone you love and trust is a liar and a fraud. The pain is indescribable, and I would not wish it on my worst enemy. And when such betrayal, deceit, and infidelity are perpetrated by a husband who pretends to be a "Man of God," the pain is even worse.

Did I suspect infidelity? Yes, and occasionally I would broach the subject with him, but Harry was adept at turning the conversation against me and to his advantage. He minimized his involvement and maximized my suspicions as figments of a wild imagination. Finally, the truth manifested itself. His adulterous behavior with numerous women in the church created such a scandal that it not only shocked the church community but threatened to split the church again and destroy me.

There were times I remember driving down Highway 620 with blinding tears of hurt flooding my eyes and spilling down my cheeks. I could hear Satan whisper in my ear, "Why do you continue to put up with this nonsense, Jan? You can easily end this misery! Just put your foot down hard on the accelerator and slightly turn the steering wheel to the left into the lane of that on-coming 18-wheeler and allow it to hit you head–on. You would be out of your misery, and it would look like an accident. Nobody would ever suspect that you did it on purpose." And then he would switch and try another approach. "No! Don't kill yourself, dummy! Just kill him!" As I struggled with those extreme suggestions swirling around in my head, the Holy Spirit would always come to my rescue by softly whispering to me my favorite Scriptures. "Trust in the Lord with all thine heart; and lean not unto thine own understanding. In all thy ways acknowledge him, and he shall direct thy paths" (Proverbs 3:5-6). "The Lord is my Shepherd: I shall not want" (Psalm 23:1). "Let not your heart be troubled: ye believe in God, believe also in me" (John 14:1). "No weapon that is formed against thee shall prosper" (Isaiah 54:17). "The Lord is my light and my salvation; whom shall I fear? The Lord is the strength of my life; of whom shall I be afraid?" (Psalm 27:1). "I can do all things through Christ which strengthens me" (Philippians 4:13)."He that dwelleth in the secret place of the most High shall abide under the shadow of the Almighty. I will say of the Lord, He is my refuge and my fortress: my God; in him will I trust" (Psalm 91:1-2). "God so loved the world that he

gave his only begotten Son, that whosoever believeth in him should not perish, but have every lasting life" (John 3:16). "Greater is he that is in you, than he that is in the world" (I John 4:4). "But they that wait upon the Lord shall renew their strength; they shall mount up with wings as eagles; they shall run, and not be weary; and they shall walk and not faint" (Isaiah 40:31). "Delight thyself also in the Lord; and he shall give thee the desires of thine heart" (Psalm 37:4). "Who shall separate us from the love of God?...For I am persuaded, that neither death, nor life, nor angels, nor principalities, nor powers, nor things present, nor things to come, nor height, nor depth, nor any other creature, shall be able to separate us from the love of God, which is in Christ Jesus our Lord" (Romans 8:35-39).

"Weeping may endure for the night, but joy cometh in the morning" (Psalm 30:5b). "Nay, in all these things we are more than conquerors through him that loved us" (Romans 8:37). And immediately an indescribable calm and clarity would sweep over me, and I knew everything would be alright.

Acknowledging Pain in Spiritual Infidelity

God Himself understands how it feels to be rejected and betrayed. Yes—God. In the Old Testament is the story of a prophet named Hosea whom God commanded to marry a prostitute. Why would God want him to do such a strange thing? Well, He wanted the nation of Israel to see what He felt when His pure love for the nation was desecrated by their worship of idols.

God wanted His chosen people to recognize their sin and to return to Him in love and reverence. After reading the Book of Hosea and experiencing my heartache, I can easily identify with God's pain.

No more intense emotion than betrayal exists. If someone had told me that my second marriage would be destroyed by adultery and infidelity, I would not have believed it. My husband was saved and trusted in the Lord Jesus Christ. More than that, he was the pastor of a growing church congregation built upon the Word of God. In fact, he even preached about preserving marriage and family. My husband loved me, and I was secure… or so I thought.

After experiencing this emotional trauma, life is never the same. One passes through a gamut of emotions—shock, denial, rage, bargaining, and despair—while mindlessly going through the mundane activities of daily life. I would not really call that "living."

Searching for a Rationale

As I contemplated what to do in the wake of my dilemma, I sought an explanation for how this could have happened. I thought long and hard about Harry's vulnerable position as pastor. Had he fallen because of the women with whom he spent time alone counseling? Some of these women were lonely, troubled, and confused. Others, I am convinced, were conniving home wreckers. I came to the conclusion that Harry was filling a need for these women that he had no right to fill. I believe that there was a definite physical attraction on both sides. Harry had a presence and an attractive manliness that made women "melt." Even men were attracted to his personality and leadership skills, and they held him in high esteem. He was a unique and appealing individual.

At first, Harry had devoted the majority of his time to prayer, sermon writing, Bible study, and the administration of the church. He had counseled females only occasionally. As time passed, however, more of his day was spent counseling, and less devoted to the Word of God in study and sermon preparations. I felt that he was spending more time with his counseling than with me and his family. I nursed twinges of jealousy in my heart, but I reminded myself that he was doing the work of God. Surely he would not want to compromise their relationship, and as far as our marriage, we had a solid relationship built on love and trust. We were a family who prayed together, worshiped together, played together, took time out to have a honeymoon every year, and did all of the things recommended to keep the home fires burning brightly. I should have realized that I was putting my trust in Harry rather than in God. You see, Harry believed that he was above reproach simply because of the title he held.

He allowed other interests to chip away at time he should have given his Bible study and sermon preparation. Harry often stayed in his study where he would listen to explicit novels on tape. Although they were not pornographic in the fullest sense of the word, nonetheless, they were explicit in their sexual content. Harry became addicted to this lewd entertainment.

Impending Danger

I learned of Harry's adultery directly from him. One evening at home, he sat me down and confessed that he had had an affair with a woman in his church. He explained that even though he loved me, he found this other woman attractive, and he violated both God and me. According to him, it was a singular act, and it would not happen again. He asked for my forgiveness, and wanted to know if we could rebuild our relationship after this affair.

If there is one weakness I have, it is blind love and trust. I loved Harry too much, and because he begged and assured me that he was not serious about this woman, I told him that I was willing to try. In reality, Harry's infidelity was so much deeper than that single act to which he had confessed. Harry's betrayal of me was wrong, but more importantly, he violated God's divine order for marriage. He was senior pastor of a growing church, and his thoughtlessness and immorality would have serious consequences—for others as well as us.

Looking back, I realize that Harry never felt any real remorse. He simply wanted me to continue to support him in the ministry. Both my womanhood and my self-confidence had been shattered. Also, there were the insecurities within my soul. What did I lack that my husband had to seek in other women? And then the shame began to emerge. As First Lady, how could I ever again hold my head up with dignity in front of a congregation that was eighty-five to ninety percent female? Had they known about these affairs all along?

Was I the only one left unaware? How long had they known, and what were they thinking about me, their pastor, and my family? The embarrassment, the criticizing eyes, and the wagging tongues were overpowering.

Maybe because Harry was blind from birth, I felt it would have been virtually impossible for him to stray. After all, if he were going to have an affair, the woman would have to pursue him, right? She would have to initiate and plan the rendezvous. He may have been able to do a lot of things by himself, but driving was not one of them. Because of his blindness, I had given him a longer leash of consideration than I probably would have if he had been sighted.

The Burning Desire to Know

Once I was confronted with the truth, I demanded to know who it was. Initially, he refused to tell me, having the nerve to say that it was not important since it was over, and it wasn't going to happen again. I demanded to know her name, and when he finally revealed who it was, I was not surprised. Despite his blindness, he had an uncanny knack for picking out physically attractive females, and they were mysteriously drawn to him. The woman in question was especially attractive, so I was not surprised that it was she. What hurt me most, however, was that I was not as attractive as she was. I had other qualities that she lacked, but she was prettier. I screamed, cried, and then I went totally silent.

When I *did* speak, I told Harry that I could not forgive him. Eventually, I began to struggle with my unwillingness to forgive, but I stood firm. Despite my private stance, I had supported and defended my husband at church. (What made it all the more difficult was my ordeal with my unfaithful husband came around the same time that President Clinton and First Lady Hillary were going through their ordeal over Monica Lewinsky). One reason I never seriously considered divorcing Harry, despite the numerous accusations of having illicit affairs, was that I never wanted to give those women who tried to break up my home the satisfaction of thinking that they had succeeded in destroying my family. I was glad that Hillary didn't divorce Bill. The haters didn't win.

On the surface, it appeared that Harry was really sorry about his infidelity. He promised to change, and I really thought that he would. I did not realize at the time, however, that Harry did not want to change, and more importantly, he had no intentions of rectifying his sin. Although he considered himself a Christian, I don't think he ever completely embraced God's vision of marriage. To him, adultery was not a serious sin against God or an act of betrayal against me. He knew if he confessed his sins, God would forgive him, and so he had turned God's compassion into a license for adultery. Harry twisted God's words and used Scripture to justify his misdeeds.

Now that our marital covenant was breached, my trust in Harry vanished. Without trust, what does a couple have? There can be no rich intimacy or true fulfillment or sustaining joy. Always lurking in my mind was the question, "Why?" I knew that I could never trust Harry again. Although my first marriage had been a continuous battleground, at least Vincent had not been a hypocrite. He may have been unsaved, bipolar, OCD, and violent, but there had never been any pretenses or masquerades. Harry, on the other hand, was a sociopath who was clever enough to convince others that he was a God-fearing man. Nothing could have been further from the truth.

It may sound strange, but I suffered more from Harry's deception and psychological abuse than I ever did from Vincent's physical violence. With Vincent, I was fully aware that I had done all I could to save our marriage and that it was utterly impossible to live with a person like him. Harry, on the other hand, would preach stirring and uplifting sermons while leading a life of hypocrisy and deceit.

Now, back to Hosea, who demonstrated how God felt when His people deserted Him and broke His heart. This biblical book is not about what to do in marriage when somebody cheats. No, it is about God's amazing love for us and His grace and mercy. We don't deserve the love that God has for us, but He continues to love and forgive us the way that He wants us to love and forgive others. And so I continued to love and forgive Harry.

But the Lord was with Jan...

almost too good to be true

Oh, taste and see that the Lord is good.

Psalm 34:8 (KJV)

An Overwhelming Response

The recent turmoil in my personal life had finally come to an end, and spiritual life at Sweet Water Baptist Church had returned to normal. It was April and time to make plans for Vacation Bible School 2000. Our pastor had been making regular announcements about the program for weeks, and the response from the parish had been tremendous. Adult volunteers (including professionals and non-professionals from all walks of life) eagerly signed up to help. Several members even took leave from their day and evening jobs so that they could come out to work with the youth. Parents who ordinarily waited until the last possible moment to sign up were lining up in the hall each week to ensure that their children would have a spot in the event.

Harry and I had solicited financial assistance and donations from various businesses, and we had enough materials donated that we could accommodate not only participants from our own church but also those from other churches in the community. Parents were encouraged to bring their children and stay for adult VBS classes, since free baby-sitting services and fun Bible review games would be available. This would be a Vacation Bible School to remember.

Ready, Set, Go!

I had prayed that God would bless this venture in a miraculous way. By the third week in June, we were ready to roll. Teachers had been recruited and trained, and lessons had been developed and distributed. The culinary ministry had planned the daily menus for over one hundred students each day of the week. The registration process, certificates, and gifts had been designed and produced on-site. Church bus drivers had been recruited, and driver records and insurance plans had been checked. We even had recess/playground helpers who knew which games to play to burn off all of the excess energy accumulated while sitting in classes for several hours. The utmost level of care had been given to every detail, and no area had been overlooked.

This was my dream come true. I don't think that I had ever been happier or more fulfilled in my life. It felt as though I had finally found my purpose and passion in life. I was a woman on fire for the Lord.

The Summons to Pastor's Office

During one of the many planning sessions in the day or two before Vacation Bible School kicked off, my husband's administrative assistant interrupted to tell me that he needed to speak to me in his study at my earliest convenience. I cheerfully responded, "Tell Pastor I will be there immediately."

I was so excited to share the great news about the preparations for Vacation Bible School because I thought Harry would be pleased and excited, too.

One time he had commented that I was the best employee he had. That compliment was meaningful to me because Harry didn't give compliments often. While he wanted others to recognize his efforts and contributions, rarely did he respond in kind. It was all a part of his personality. He didn't mean any harm by it; it was just that his philosophy was to give praises sparingly so that people would work harder to receive them. Therefore, pleasing my husband was one of my biggest goals. Vacation Bible School was coming together well, and I was hoping to receive his thanks and compliments.

Actions Speak Louder Than Words

As I entered Harry's study, I saw him standing behind his desk and looking extremely sharp in his white shirt and dark tie. The thought crossed my mind that even after so many years had passed, he still looked handsome to me. Still, there was something strange about his manner. He stood rigidly like a drill sergeant with his arms folded across his chest. I thought it a very strange stance for what should have been a happy occasion.

I dismissed the thought as quickly as it had come and excitedly related the news about Vacation Bible School.

"Honey, VBS is going great this year! Have you had time to see the good things that are going on? I think that this is going to be the best summer Bible program we have had in our church's history. Aren't you thrilled?"

I was talking a mile a minute and was so happy and excited that I didn't hear him when he said, "Sit down. We need to talk."

It still hadn't registered. Then, all of a sudden, he shouted at me in a harsh tone, "Sit down, and be quiet! I need to talk to you about something very important!"

It was only then that I realized that Harry was not interested in what was going on with Vacation Bible School or any other church-related matter. No, Harry had something entirely different on his mind, and whatever it was, it was not going to be good news. I braced myself for something horrible. I didn't know what else to do, so I just stood rooted to the spot— dumbfounded. Then the man that I loved and had married nearly twenty-two years earlier coldly spoke words that would change my life forever.

He said to me, "I'm sorry, but this marriage is over. I don't love you anymore, and I am getting a divorce."

But the Lord is still with Jan...

betrayal, rejection, and a little touch of insanity

But thou hast utterly rejected us; thou are very wroth against us.

Lamentations 5:22 (KJV)

Blindsided–Never Saw It Coming

A "matter of great importance" changed my life forever. What Harry had to tell me was, "I don't love you anymore, and I am getting a divorce. Our marriage is over!"

Huh! What did he say?

"I don't love you anymore, and I am getting a divorce. Our marriage is over!" This had to be some weird, sick joke. I couldn't believe my ears! The sting of my husband's words made my heart skip several beats. If Harry had slapped me hard across my face with the back of his open hand as hard as he could, he couldn't have hurt me more. I felt I was having a heart attack. There was great pain and pressure in my chest, as if an elephant were sitting on me. I could hardly breathe, and nausea and faintness came at the same time. As I fought to regain my breath, Harry continued to talk, completely oblivious to what his words were doing to me. He continued spewing out venom, saying how he was going to get rid of me, throw me out of his house, and trade me in for a younger model. His words cut through me like a dagger, and yet I continued to stand there—shocked, in disbelief, frozen and bewildered, and too dazed to blink or move.

While he spoke, his words were sucking the life out of my body and ripping me to shreds, yet those same words never seemed to faze Harry in the least. Finally, he ceased talking about his "matter of great importance," and then he did something that hammered the nails of my coffin shut. Harry calmly turned away from his desk, coolly walked over and picked up his cap and suit jacket from the coat rack standing in the corner of his office, and walked out of his study into his administrative assistant's office. He informed her that he was leaving for the day, and if anyone needed to see the pastor, they could contact him at home. And with those words, he disappeared from view, and his deacon/driver drove him home.

Stunned, Dazed, and Overcome

I don't remember how long I stood there in the middle of the pastor's study, but it seemed like forever. I just continued to stand. I couldn't move. I was totally trau-matized by what he had said to me. I don't think I will ever forget his words. "I don't love you anymore, and I am getting a divorce. Our marriage is over!"

I continued to replay the scene in my mind. Slowly, the reality of what had just happened began to sink in, and the blows from the cruelty of his words made me stagger backward. I collapsed onto the couch behind me in his study. And still I couldn't believe my ears.

"I don't love you anymore, and I am getting a divorce. Our marriage is over!" If words could kill, I was now a corpse. It could not have been any worse for me than if my pastor/husband had stood across the room in front of me, pulled out a revolver, and shot me at point blank range. His words pierced me in a way that was far deeper and greater than mere bullets from a gun could have.

The Sting of Treachery and Duplicity

"I don't love you anymore, and I am getting a divorce. Our marriage is over!" I couldn't get the words out of my mind! The pain, heartache, and devastation were more than I could bear.

It's strange, but even though I was frozen in disbe-lief and was slowly being driven off a precipitous cliff, I still couldn't take his words seriously. I dared not take them seriously. My mind would not have been able to cope if those words were true. I had to reject what had happened.

I had to be dreaming. Yes, this was some big, terrible nightmare—some horrible, twisted, and ghastly mistake. Or maybe I had been sleepwalking and I would soon wake up from this nightmare. That's it. I had to wake up.

But it was no dream. It wasn't a mistake. What happened was real. Harry had meant every word he said because he meant to hurt me and hurt me badly. But why? What had I ever done but love and cherish him as my husband. I didn't understand. And all the while his words continued reverberating in my head.

"I don't love you anymore, and I am getting a divorce. Our marriage is over!"

"I don't love you anymore, and I am getting a divorce. Our marriage is over!"

"I don't love you anymore, and I am getting a divorce. Our marriage is over!"

Your Mind is a Terrible Thing to Lose

I was slowly losing my mind as I sat there on the couch in the pastor's study that summer day in June, 2000. I believe I temporarily went insane from the post-traumatic shock of those toxic words.

Not only did I begin talking to myself and asking myself questions, but I began answering myself out loud, as well. As I sat on that couch in his study, I analyzed what had just happened to me. I acted like a prosecuting attorney and a big city police chief downtown at some precinct somewhere. I was talking and answering myself like some insane, demented, crazy woman.

"Jan!"

"Yes!" I said to myself.

"Jan, tell me, what just happened, and why are you so surprised at this? Hadn't you seen this coming? Why were you so completely caught off guard? Didn't you notice anything that should have prepared you for this trauma/drama/ordeal? Think, girl. Speak up, Jan!"

And I answered myself, "Uhhh, well, yes, I think I did notice some clues now that you press me."

Then I said to myself, "Good, Jan. What were some of the clues that should have given you a 'heads-up'?"

I answered myself, "Well, to tell you the truth, I had begun to suspect that something was not right years ago."

"Really, Jan?"

"Yes, I am not what you could call psychic or anything like that, but I had started to perceive that there were little things going wrong that I didn't like to think about."

"Little things? Such as what, Jan?"

"Well, there were his mannerisms, for instance. He seemed nervous and antsy a lot of the time."

"Really now?"

"Yes!" I said to myself, "and he wasn't as warm and affectionate toward me as he used to be in the beginning. I had sensed a change in his behavior for some time."

"How interesting, Jan. When did you first begin to notice these changes?"

"It's strange, but I do believe the real changes started to occur right after he graduated from seminary and received his doctorate degree in 1994."

"Uhhh… that is remarkable! What do you think caused this change in his behavior toward you, Jan?"

"Well, I am not really sure, but it seemed to me as if he had accomplished his goal, and he didn't need me as much anymore."

"I see. That is intriguing, Jan. But I don't understand. You both had made great accomplishments. You both had received your doctorate degrees. Didn't that make you feel good?"

"Ummm, well, no, I didn't receive my doctorate degree."

"What? You mean to tell me that you didn't receive that piece of paper that your dad had always said was so important? Jan, are you telling me that you went to graduate school and seminary with your husband for nearly ten years and you didn't graduate, too?"

"Ummm, that's right. I didn't graduate."

"Well, Jan, help me to understand why you didn't get your doctorate degree in Biblical Studies with your husband, silly girl."

"Well, he convinced me that it would be too expensive for the church to pay for both of our degrees. After all, he was the pastor, and the church would only pay for his. Besides, what would I do with a doctorate degree? And anyway, Harry said that I didn't need one."

"Oh, I see. And tell me this, Jan. Did you believe him when he told you that you did not need a doctorate degree?"

"Well, yes, I did. After all, he was my husband, and we were in the ministry together. He was the pastor. People were coming to church to listen to him—not me."

"But Jan, who did most of the work for this doctorate degree?"

"I did."

"Oh, I see! Exactly what work did you do to earn this doctorate degree for your pastor/husband, Jan?"

"Well, I read the textbooks along with the Bible, wrote out his assignments, spent long hours in the library looking up information, took class notes, wrote term papers, helped him get his assignments completed and recorded them on a tape recorder so that he could translate them into Braille."

"That's quite a bit of work, don't you think, Jan?

"Yes."

"Tell me this, Jan. Did you work full time teaching school during the day at the same time you were going to seminary with him in the evening?"

"Well, yes."

"Did you help him study for his test, too, Jan?"

"Yes, I did."

"Jan, tell me this. Who wrote the test questions down and answered them for him in class during the test taking time?"

"I did."

"Oh, you did. Well, Jan, tell me, did you get compensated for doing all this work for your husband?"

"No."

"Jan, why didn't the seminarian professors test your husband?"

"They said they were too busy, and I was welcomed to sit in on all the classes and serve as his eyes. God would bless me, and I would be a wonderful wife."

"Oh, really! And you fell for that, Jan?"

"Yes."

"Do you still believe him, Jan?"

"No! No! No!"

"Jan, tell me, did you have any other indications that your marriage was… let us say, deteriorating?"

"Well, he wasn't as warm and affectionate with me as he used to be."

"Oh, really? What else?"

"Well, many times he was indifferent and showed a lack of sensitivity toward me—almost disrespect."

"Ummm… what else?"

"Well, occasionally, he would embarrass me or put me down in front of members of the church. But whenever I would confront him or tell him how he hurt my feelings, he would say that he was just kidding or that I was too overly sensitive. He would tell me that I shouldn't wear my feelings on my sleeve."

"Jan, was there anything else?"

"Yes, there was more. There was a coldness building between us. We would seldom spend time together. Even when we were at home together in the same room, we were not together. This slight distance between us concerned me. I sensed ever so slightly that something was coming between us."

"Did you talk with your husband about this, Jan?"

"No!"

"Why not?"

"Because he was spending more and more time counseling other church members, so he had less and less time available for me."

"Jan, didn't you feel this was not right? What did you do about this?"

"I would confront him, but he would counter me more and more with sarcastic remarks or, at times, belittle me in front of others."

"What did you do about this, Jan?"

"I would jokingly dismiss it and chalk it up to his being fatigued or make some other excuse for him."

"Jan, I know that your husband/pastor was very particular about whom he would allow to teach the members of his congregation when he was away preaching revivals in other cities. However, since you were in seminary with your husband and you studied right along with him, surely he would allow you to teach Bible lessons in his place. After all, teaching is your spiritual gift, right?"

"Yes."

"You were more than qualified to teach the Bible lessons for him in his absence, don't you think?"

"Yes."

"Then did he allow you to substitute for him or not—when he was away?"

"No, he didn't let me teach—not even the women in the church."

"Really? Why do you think he did not let you teach for him, Jan?"

"He said that teaching was his job and that the women did not want the pastor's wife lording over them."

"Do you think that was true, Jan?

"At first I believed him, but now I am not so sure. Most of the women told me they liked the way I taught."

"I see. Tell me, didn't you write his Bible lessons?"

"Yes, but that was different. I wrote the lessons for *him*."

"Hmmm, interesting! What else do you recall about your pastor/husband, Jan?"

"Nothing!"

"Are you sure, Jan?

"Wasn't there something about his popularity with the females in the church? Weren't the phone calls at all times of the day and night increasing, and wasn't he spending more and more time away from his home and the church? Were there members who were leaving the church due to all of the innuendo and gossip about the questionable behavior of your husband with women in the congregation?"

Crossing that Fine Line

"Stop it! Stop harassing me! Oh, my goodness! I think I have totally lost my mind! I have got to stop this!"

Throughout this entire conversation, Harry's words continued to wrangle in my mind.

"I don't love you anymore, and I am getting a divorce. Our marriage is over!"

"Oh, God, please help me!"

And believe it or not, my mind checked out. I don't have any recollection of what happened next.

And the Lord was still with Jan...

"you have been sued for divorce"

"The God of Israel hates divorce" (Malachi 2:16).

The Classic Crime Scene

For the life of me, I don't remember what happened during those summer months. It's a complete blur. But I will never forget what happened that fall. The date was Monday, September 25, 2000. I was returning home, having just facilitated one of the best Sunday school teachers' meetings I have been to in a long time. As Christian Education Director, Sunday school teacher, First Lady of the Church, wife and mother all rolled into one, I finally felt that I was beginning to master the challenges of my various roles in the ministry. I believed that God's work was finally beginning to manifest itself.

Harry had called earlier that evening to tell me to hurry home. He said that there would be someone coming who needed to see me. I walked alone from the church back to my home in the serene community where I lived. I was acutely aware of my tranquil surroundings. It was a crisp, autumn evening, and stars twinkled in the night sky. A full moon shone brightly, and I could see my neighbors' perfectly manicured lawns as I passed their houses. I was energetic, upbeat, and jubilant. Life was good, and I was happy to be alive.

As I reached my house, I went in, put down my things and moved into the kitchen to wash my hands and prepare a snack for the "visitor" Harry had told me was coming by. As a pastor's wife, I was used to having something ready for anyone that might pop in unannounced. It happened all the time, and I always had plenty of goodies on hand to entertain.

The Absolute Shock of My Life

It was not long before I heard a car pull up in the driveway. Thinking that it must be the "guest," I turned on the lights in the foyer. As I opened the door, to my surprise I saw a Texas State Constable's car parked in the driveway. I was startled as I thought to myself, "Why in the world is a constable's car parked here at my house?" I knew that constables could serve warrants the same as police officers, so my curiosity was definitely peaked.

Harry was in his study, which was near the front door, but he never came out to see what was happening. By this time, the uniformed officer had reached our front door, greeted me, and asked, "Are you Jan Byrd?"

"Yes, I am," I answered cheerfully.

He pulled an envelope from his inside coat pocket and placed it in my hand. Then he said to me, "You have just been sued for divorce." Without another word, he turned, walked away, got into his marked car, and drove off. I stood frozen at the front door of my home. I couldn't move. I was in an absolute state of shock. I couldn't believe my ears. This couldn't be happening to me. Yes, he had said it, but I never actually thought he would actually go through with it.

My body went numb...as cold as ice. And I thought to myself, "So is this how it feels when you die?" The lights went out for me; my mind went blank; and I don't remember anything after that.

But the Lord was still with Jan...

God, I can't believe you said no!

"For this thing I besought the Lord thrice, that it might depart from me. And He said unto me, my grace is sufficient for thee.

2 Corinthians 12:8-9 (KJV)

I was so deeply hurt that I wanted to curl up on the floor and cry my eyes out. I knew I was the topic of gossip, leaving me in the uncomfortable position of avoiding people that I once considered friends. I wanted to cry out, "Lord, where are you when I need you the most?" Harry's demand for a divorce left me broken-hearted, crushed, and utterly defeated.

He was filing for a divorce despite the fact that he had no legal grounds to do so. He claimed that it was due to irreconcilable differences, but it sounded like, "I have someone younger and better, so I'm trading you in for a newer model." While I was over ten years older than Harry, it should not have made a bit of difference to someone who had sworn before God to spend the rest of his life with me. When I asked Harry what he would say when he stood before God on Judgment Day, he arrogantly replied, "I'll take my chances." Here was a preacher who wasn't even afraid of God.

Too Strong for My Own Good

Even though I was tremendously worried during this period in my life, I never even told my own children about the emotional pain and heartache that I was suffering. I knew they could not understand how I felt. I was looked upon as a strong woman in the Lord; however, that was not true. I bottled up my feelings, and as a result, no one offered comfort and support. My friends and members of the church must have felt that I was strong enough to handle this set-back in my life. Everyone thought more highly of me than they should have, but it was my fault since I hadn't shared my feelings with them. Each day, I put on my bravest face and went about my routine as if nothing had changed. I awoke early, went to work, taught my class at school, and returned home. As a matter of fact, my weary act was so good that my colleagues at Grant Elementary School nominated me for "Teacher of the Year." Though I was going through the motions of living, I was dying inside. No one had any idea that I was losing my hold on life.

Praying without Ceasing

Finally, I did what I should have been doing all along— I prayed. I tried to break down the doors of heaven with my prayers, relying on my faith (no larger than a mustard seed) to turn things around. I was certain that God would save my marriage. After all, He created marriage even before the church. He performed the first wedding in the Garden of Eden, and according to Malachi 2:16, He hates divorce. Scripture says that if you pray believing, you will receive what you ask for. So I prayed with Psalm 37:4 on my lips. "Delight thyself also in the Lord; and He shall give you the desires of thine heart." He always answers prayer in one of three ways: yes, no, or wait—and He will always answer. I was positive that God was going to give me the reconciliation that I was begging him for.

Desperate Times Call for Desperate Measures

While I believe in prayer, I sometimes get the urge to "help God out" a little. That's why I was determined to fight for my marriage of more than twenty years. How could a Christian marriage be so easily destroyed by the Devil's lies and misconceptions? I did my best to hang on to my husband. I cooked all of his favorite meals, and I even got up at four in the morning to exercise with him (despite the fact that I do not like to exercise, and I definitely do not like the thought of exercising early in the morning). Some mornings, I even suggested that the two of us walk around the neighborhood to help his cholesterol levels. When he got angry and said he was leaving, I replied, "Good, I'll go with you," while proceeding to pack my bags and wait for us to leave.

He would get angry, change his mind, and say, "I'm not leaving. You are." At times like this, he would remind me that the church was paying the mortgage for him and not me; therefore, I had to leave. I paid him no mind.

You might be thinking, *Girl! You're nuts! Why didn't you just accept the inevitable and let the man go?* You are absolutely right, but I felt that I had to fight for what was mine—and fight I did. What others thought about me didn't matter, and I didn't care how undignified I might have looked. I didn't care who called me a foolish woman. I didn't care about any of that. The only thing important to me was saving my marriage and the husband I loved. What God had joined was sacred to me and was not going to be undone by other women or even a husband going through his mid-life crisis. I had no intention of releasing him from his marital vows without a struggle. There was a slim possibility that God would set him straight, but more than anything else, I didn't want to have regrets later, thinking that if I had just tried harder perhaps things might have worked themselves out.

The Big Letdown

After all of that effort, did God give me the answer to my prayer that I had hoped for? He didn't. On March 26, 2001, the divorce became final, and my world caved in. I asked God, "Why did you let me down like this? I can't believe you said 'No!'"

God responded to my despair, "I *did* answer your prayer but not in the way that you wanted me to. You didn't have a marriage—you had a mess. I love you too much to say yes to something that is not good for you."

The Sufficiency of God's Grace

I still couldn't believe that God would treat me this way. I cried big, gut-wrenching sobs until I could barely breathe. I was angry with God because I felt that He had been mean to me, but I was also astonished and confused. Never in my wildest dreams did I expect that God would treat me like this. I opened my Bible and began to read from God's Word—just as I had every time that life left me bewildered.

As I turned the pages, tears blinded my eyes, and it was difficult for me to focus, but it was as if God's arms were wrapped around me, leading me to 2 Corinthians 12. As I read the familiar story about Paul, I felt the tension give way to calm and peace.

Even though I had read this chapter before, it was as if I were reading it for the very first time. It was amazing. Paul, that great man of faith, had prayed for God to answer a prayer—just like me. Paul prayed three times for God to remove the debilitating infirmity in his body, but God refused. God had actually said no to this great, faithful servant of his. Paul had prayed hard, too, like me, trying to reason with God that if He removed the sickness, he could do a better job for Him. It was a reasonable request, and I agreed with Paul. But I now realized something that I had not earlier. I learned that even though God loved Paul very much, He had a reason for saying no. God needed to humble Paul so that His servant could learn firsthand and then teach others that God's grace is all we need. It fascinated me that Christ told Paul in such plain words, "My grace is sufficient for thee: for my strength is made perfect in weakness" (2 Corinthians 12:9). Paul was brought down to his knees in weakness, and yet it was that very weakness that carried him on to his greatest success and spiritual victory. Paul learned that in his weakness, Jesus Christ would be able to live more fully in him, and God would give Paul the very strength that he needed to accomplish what he could not do himself. When Paul reached this epiphany, he wrote the immortal words found in 2 Corinthians 12:9. "Then I would rather boast in my infirmities, that the power of Christ may rest upon me."

I dried my tears and began feeling much better. Maybe God wanted to do something similar with me. Could God be trying to teach me about His amazing grace and mercy through my suffering and pain? Perhaps God was preparing me to serve as a blessing to others by carrying me through this ordeal. I wasn't sure. Later, as I reflected on what I had read, I felt ashamed of my anger toward God, and I asked Him to forgive me. He did (1 John 1:9). Paul's verses became an anchor for my soul during those difficult times, and although my heart was still heavy with the pain of my loss, I knew that God would eventually give me beauty for my ashes (Isaiah 61:3).

And the Lord was with Jan...

PART FOUR:
healing and renewal

divorced, but no longer devastated

You shall know them by their fruits. Every good tree brings forth good fruit; but a corrupt tree brings forth evil fruit

Matthew 7:16-17 (KJV)

Defining the Indefinable

What is divorce? Divorce is the shattering of one's dreams, hopes, and aspirations. It is a living nightmare that not only breaks the heart but disrupts life's plans. Divorce is the antithesis of heaven. It is a synonym for hell. It is one of life's devastating tragedies.

Different Philosophies

Divorce was life-changing and catastrophic for me. However, I realize that it does not have the same effect on everyone. For example, I have an attractive girlfriend with a gorgeous body, shapely legs, a ready smile, a quick wit, and a brilliant mind. Men are just naturally drawn to her. This friend has been married and divorced several times, but unlike me, she has never been dejected or overly depressed about it. On the contrary, she seems to carry on with her life in a wholesome and positive way. Divorce may have adversely affected her internally, but she has never shown it on the outside. She feels that life is too short to be miserable. Her philosophy is, "Men are like busses. If you don't like the ride on one, get off at the next stop and catch another."

Yes, I liked that philosophy, but that philosophy didn't work for me.

My marriage number one dissolved because it was doomed from the start. It is quite obvious to me now that I did not use my head and select wisely at the age of nineteen. From the very beginning, Vincent was bipolar and had OCD (Obsessive-Compulsive Disorder, an anxiety disorder characterized by repetitive behaviors and compulsions). In addition to his obsessions, he was violent. No one can live safely in a violent atmosphere. I had to divorce him to survive. Yes, I know what you are thinking. No one in her right mind would have contemplated marriage in the first place. Common sense should have warned me not to marry him. I now understand the adage, "Common sense is not so common." In fact, it is extremely rare. Maybe I should not have married husband number one, but what about husband number two? Who would have imagined that Harry, my God-fearing (or so I thought), church going, witnessing, Bible reading preacher would trade me in for a younger model? Well, *I* didn't. I was totally devastated by this second divorce. I believed life was over for me, and I felt there was no place for this divorced woman in ministry.

Becoming a Fruit Inspector

The hardest part of ministry for me was discerning who was real in the body of Christ. His Word tells us not to judge another person because we are limited in our knowledge. We can only look at the outside of a person and see the visible and transparent. Only God can see and read the heart of an individual. But God wanted to teach me how to examine the fruit produced by each tree. My earthly assignment was to become a spiritual fruit inspector.

You and I can always judge a tree by its fruit. If the fruit is good, the tree is good. If the fruit is rotten, it's because the tree is rotten. A good tree will not produce bad fruit, and a bad tree can never produce good fruit. Time is the key. Sooner or later, the truth will be revealed. I learned not to judge but to just wait and test the fruit. The pretenders looked like Christians, talked like Christians, and walked like Christians until the storm arose in the church. Then their true "colors" came forth. What was written on the tablet of their hearts became evident. Sadly, more Christians are wounded by "friendly fire" in the ministry than in all the wars of history. It is true that church folks often "shoot" their wounded by the slip of the tongue.

Recognizing Bad Fruit

I did not realize it at the time, but there were a few church sisters who were less than sympathetic about my divorce. A few of them, I came to learn, had envied me in the past because they wanted to be a preacher's wife. Why? I really don't know. If only they had known what life was really like for me. The charlatans came out when the storms of life were pounding on the victim. These phony sisters were like parasites and vampires, lurking around to suck every ounce of blood left from the devastation inflicted by the divorce.

Therefore, very few embraced me at this desperate time of need in my life. Many wouldn't talk with me; they just stared and wagged those vicious tongues. Very few had words of comfort and consolation because I was the "First Lady," and I didn't need anything from them. They may outwardly have appeared to be saddened by my loss, but inwardly they were enjoying every morsel of my hurt, sorrow, and devastation. There were wheat and tares growing up together. Both were in the house of God.

Discerning Good Fruit

Sooner or later, the Holy Spirit would reveal to me the true identity of each sister in the church. Oh, I thank God for my numerous true sisters in the body of Christ who embraced me at this desperate time of need. Many of them didn't come to me personally, but I could feel their prayers and in their eyes I could see their kind thoughts of sympathy. They will never know how their prayers and affection for me kept me going. From them, I gained strength to go on in the face of my desperation and devastation. These precious sisters of Sweet Water Baptist Church saved my life, and I will be forever grateful to them. Their love and silent prayers kept me afloat when I could have drowned in despair and hopelessness.

Alone but Not Lonely

Despite my many failures, Jesus still loves me, died, and rose again for me. And anyone who had a problem with me, then that was their problem—not mine. God loves me. I may not have a husband, but I have a peace and contentment that I never had in either marriage. I may be living alone, but I am not lonely. I am single yet totally satisfied. Jesus has shown me that He has a powerful ministry for me—not in spite of my divorces—but maybe because of my brokenness and messed up marriages. Jesus loves me! Yes, He does. I know because the Bible tells me so!

And the Lord was with Jan...

forgiveness is an inside job

"If you forgive men their sins against you, your heavenly Father will also forgive you. But if you do not forgive men their sins, your Father will not forgive your sins" (Matthew 6:14-15, KJV).

Doing What's Right Ain't Easy

One of the fundamental truths of Christianity is that we must forgive those who have hurt us, but the more deeply one is hurt, the more difficult it is to forgive. When one has been rejected, betrayed, and deceived, it becomes almost impossible to know where to begin.

Forgiveness has been a big struggle for me. Why should I be forced to forgive two men who caused me so much pain and misery for so many years? The very thought of forgiving those two rascals makes me ill. I feel exploited, humiliated, and demoralized. I just can't seem to bring myself to forgive them. Worst of all, I don't know if the problem is that I don't know how to forgive or that I just don't want to. Ultimately, I know I must release my poisonous thoughts of wicked revenge, but, please, not just yet. I am not ready to forgive! I am having too much fun thinking of ways to get even!

Domestic Violence and Psychological Abuse is a Two-Sided Coin

On one side of the coin is physical abuse, which is easy to detect. Many times, the physical abuse leaves behind tell-tale signs of visible scars—maybe even broken bones.

On the other side of the coin is psychological and emotional abuse, which is not as easily detected with the naked eye... or by x-ray machines. The damage is more difficult to diagnose because scars are internal. I endured both kinds of abuse.

Heads: Domestic Violence with Vincent

Tell me, how do I forgive Vincent? How do I forgive a man who subjected me to domestic violence for nearly twenty years due to his bipolar and obsessive-compulsive disorder? How do I forgive a man who systematically isolated me from friends, family, and co-workers and lost his temper, had explosively violent outbursts if I did not agree with everything he said or did, kept his children and me walking around the house as if on eggshells, hit me, went into my closet and ripped up my clothing, shook and threw me around like a rag doll, gave me the silent treatment for weeks at a time and then, without notice, began yelling and calling me every bad name in the book? Tell me, how do I forgive a man who was jealous of any tiny bit of success I achieved on my job until I felt it necessary to hide in the back hall closet or in the trunk of my car the numerous Christmas gifts I received yearly from my students so that he would not see them and have an angry fit because he had not received any gifts from his students at school?

Tell me, how do I forgive a man who worried me to the point that most of my hair fell out and my skin broke out in hives and my weight dropped to less than ninety-five pounds? Only the good Lord kept me sane and in relatively good health. Tell me, how do I forgive a husband who constantly belittled me—all in the name of "keeping me grounded and humble?" How do I forgive and forget that kind of misery? Tell me, because I really want to know.

Tails: Emotional and Psychological Abuse with Harry

Tell me, how do I forgive Harry? We were married for over twenty years, and even though he never laid a hand on me, I find it is easier to forgive Vincent than Harry; at least Vincent was not saved and did not know the Lord when I married him. At the tender age of nineteen, I simply didn't have the wisdom to select a man who could be a good husband and father. Ignorance is not bliss, and it cost me and my children dearly. Harry, on the other hand, was supposed to be different. He was a born-again Christian who not only knew the Word of God, but preached it to others.

How do I forgive Harry, who used me to obtain his goals in life, including attending seminary and receiving his doctoral degree? Tell me, how do I forgive a "preacher man" who controlled everything, made all of the important decisions, monopolized our time together, and made sure that it was always about *him* and never *us*? Tell me, how do I forgive a pastor-husband who twisted Scripture to constantly remind me that man is the head of the woman and that I should obey him explicitly and "stay in my appointed place"? Tell me, how do I forgive a man who stripped me of my dignity by forcing me to listen as woman after woman came forth in the business meetings to tell the church about their inappropriate behavior with my husband/pastor? Tell me, how do I forgive him for humiliating and demoralizing his wife, daughter, elderly grandmother, mother-in-law, and his loyal church members who trusted and believed in him in such a public forum as a church business meeting? How do I forgive a man who tells me he has no grounds for divorcing me, but he is going to trade me in for a younger model? How do I forgive a pastor-husband who not only divorced me but dismissed God and his ministry, as well? How do I forgive Harry, but more importantly, how do I forgive my own stupidity?

Revenge Can be Sweet

Vengeance is the Lord's, and I know that. But there are times when I would like to put the Bible aside and reap sweet revenge on my two ex-husbands. Just for a little while, I would like to pay them back for how deeply they hurt me. I wouldn't want to torture them Guantanamo-style or beat them within an inch of their lives, but I would like for them to experience the awful pain of rejection that I experienced at their hands. After all, Christians are human, too. My fantasies of revenge have been delicious and satisfying, just the same.

Knowing What to Do Is
Not the Same as Doing It

Spiritually speaking, I knew it did not matter how badly my ex-husbands had treated me. I knew I had to forgive them. The Lord's Prayer told me that God would forgive me in direct proportion to how I forgave my debtors. If I did not forgive Harry and Vincent, then the Lord would not forgive me. Even though I wanted the Lord to forgive me for my stupidity, I sometimes felt that it was too hard for me to forgive those two men. Forgiving is easier said than done because I felt I had earned the right to hold a grudge against them. Worse still, even if I forced myself to say that I forgave them, it wouldn't be from my heart. I might have been able to fool Vincent and Harry for a while, but I wouldn't fool God for one minute. The Lord sees everything, and He would know that I was insincere. Therefore, I was in a real dilemma, until I went to my Bible and read Isaiah 53 again. I needed to know how Jesus had forgiven those who had sinned against Him. I had a serious problem, and I needed help.

What Did Jesus Do?

After I read Isaiah 53, I understood more clearly what Jesus had done for me. He loved me enough to leave the magnificence of heaven, come down to earth, and become one like me. Jesus was without beauty and had no majesty or grace to draw my eyes and make me delight in Him. Jesus came unto His own, but His own received Him not. He was despised and rejected of men. Yet He bore my torments, and He was smitten by God. Jesus was pierced for my transgressions and tortured for my iniquities. His suffering was for my salvation. For me, He was scourged so that I could be healed. I had strayed. Like a sheep, I had gone my own way, but the Father God laid upon His only begotten Son all my guilt (Isaiah 53:6). Jesus submitted to be struck down and did not open His mouth, allowing himself to be led to the slaughter just for me. Without protection and without justice, Jesus died for me. As He was dying on that cross, He forgave me because He loved me with a perfect agape love. That's amazing.

After reading Isaiah 53, I clearly understood why I could no longer reject God's biblical mandate to forgive my former husbands. What a loving example my Heavenly Father had given me through His only begotten Son Jesus Christ.

Forgiveness Brings Freedom

Jesus's unconditional love for me enabled me to do the impossible. With God, all things are possible (Matthew

19:26). He taught me that forgiveness emanated from the inside out and that I had the grace to forgive both Harry and Vincent. It was just a matter of the will. God had not held me hostage for what I have done to Him, and now I needed to release my ex-husbands from the prison of my mind. Amazingly, as soon as I forgave both men, I became liberated. I felt as free as a bird. My anger and bitterness melted away, and the doors of my self-imposed prison sprang open. I learned that forgiveness is liberating. I could begin to think about my future instead of my negative past. What a positive change.

My Heavenly Father taught me another important lesson. Forgiveness is not synonymous with approval. Forgiving Harry and Vincent did not mean that I approved of or excused what they had done to me. There are those who refuse to forgive because they feel that forgiveness is a sign of weakness, but it is not. Forgiveness is a sign of strength. Forgiveness is powerful because it must come from the heart. Forgiveness is an inside job.

And the Lord was with Jan...

a move of faith: journey of a restored woman

But without faith it is impossible to please him, for he who comes to God must believe that He is, and that He is a rewarder of those who diligently seek Him.

Hebrews 11:6 (KJV)

Ambivalent Emotions

Next week, I'll be starting a new chapter in my life by leaving Round Rock, Texas, to move to Greenville, North Carolina. Many have asked me how I feel about my move. I am ambivalent. Part of me is eager to be closer to my granddaughters, Cheyenne and Blair, and my son and daughter-in-law, Lawrence and Nicole, but another part of me is dreading the disruption.

I know that God has called me to move, yet I am sad about leaving close friends, associates, my job, my church family, and Pastor, Gaylon C. Clark at Greater Mt. Zion Baptist Church in Austin, Texas. I have become so content and comfortable with my life here, and embracing the unknown is frightening, to say the least. I believe that the older one becomes, the more difficult it is to make such drastic changes.

Biblical Characters Relocated, Too

I reflect upon how Abraham must have felt when God told him to move into the unknown at the age of seventy-five. By our standards, he would have been a senior citizen on social security for over ten years. I am nearly seventy and find that it is extremely difficult for me, but even as I give tribute to Father Abraham, it is his dear and faithful wife Sarah that I especially admire. I can imagine how she must have felt, leaving to follow a husband who had "heard a call from God."

Sarah loved her husband, and if he was going to pack up and leave for the unknown because he had heard from Almighty God, she was going to accompany him. To me, Sarah had more faith than Abraham. She never heard from God, yet her faith was blind and true—not to mention that God was with them every step of the way.

At the age of sixty-five, when Sarah should have been thinking about settling down and enjoying the fruits of her labors, she was undertaking an epic journey. The couple endured struggles and disappointments, but the good overcame the bad. Sarah became the mother of Isaac at the age of ninety, which shows that even when her trip was over, her journey with God was not. She even made it into Hebrews chapter 11, which is a biblical "Hall of Fame" of sorts. She and Rahab, the Harlot, are the only other women in that entire list of heroes.

What was Abe talking about? He said God had talked with him and told him to move. But God never talked to Sarah. How did she know that her husband wasn't having a late-life crisis? Until that time, only Enoch and Noah had ever communicated directly with God, and everybody knows what happened to each of them. Enoch walked and talked with God, and the next thing we know, he was no more. Everyone looked high and low for him, but he was never found. Moses wrote that God was so pleased with Enoch that He took him to His house in heaven. And then there was Noah who heard the voice of God and began building an ark and preaching a four word sermon "It's going to Rain!" Rain? What's rain? It had never rained before! Noah must have been considered the worst preacher ever, because he preached that same old tired sermon for one hundred twenty years and never won a single convert (unless you count his wife, three sons, and their three wives). Everybody else thought Noah was out of his mind. But it *did* rain! Then everyone wanted to join Noah on the ark, but it was too late. God had shut the door and locked Noah and his family inside with all the animals.

Sometimes I waver a little in my thinking. Maybe God didn't tell me to relocate. Maybe I've just misheard Him. Maybe I shouldn't be stepping out on faith like this. Maybe I'm making a tremendous mistake. But, at times like this, I think of Sarah, one of my biblical heroes. Sarah was no "spring chicken" when she had Isaac, but she had faith enough to trust God. Wow! Sarah is my inspiration; she gives me the will to follow the Lord, as He leads the way.

Hearing and Responding to My Call

It was while driving from Dallas to Round Rock in 1988 after Harry became pastor of Sweet Water Baptist Church that I first received my call from God. If you recall, I had stayed behind to complete my final year of teaching in Dallas and sell our home. It was during one of those three-hour drives to see Harry that God clearly spoke to me concerning ministry. The Lord wanted me to share His words of wisdom with accuracy, clarity, simplicity, and maybe even a bit of humor. I could see myself standing before large audiences and proclaiming the Word of God. In my vision I saw millions coming to know Jesus Christ—men, women, boys and girls. I shared my vision with Harry, but he was not the least bit impressed or encouraging. He said to me in a matter-of-fact way, "God didn't call you to preach. What you experienced while driving was indigestion from eating junk food on the road. Women who say they are called to preach are just frustrated females who can't get a man, but you aren't like them." Oddly enough, Harry's words weren't said in a mean or condemning way. He almost made it sound as if he were paying me a compliment. Then he quickly changed the subject, but I never forgot God's call. I simply placed it on the back burner of my mind.

From then on, Harry would allow me to teach occasionally at Sweet Water, but for the most part, I remained an untapped resource. Once Pastor Harry had realized that the women received my teaching so eagerly, he completely refrained from asking me to teach. However, he did let me teach the youth during Sunday school but never the women in the church. It was not until after the divorce and my tedious search of many months for a church home, that I was led to Greater Mount Zion Church in Austin. The church's young and dynamic spiritual leaders, Pastor Gaylon C. Clark and the First Lady Kathy, both welcomed me with opened arms. The entire Greater Mt. Zion membership reached out and accepted me without condemnation or criticism. I felt secure and safe.

Pastor Clark began to develop my spiritual gifts. With his mentoring and encouragement, it was not long before I was teaching in the Women's Ministry with the dynamic Michele Pearson. I will forever be grateful for Pastor Clark's nurturing, coming as it did when I felt useless and incapable of doing anything special for the Lord or anyone else. They accepted me for who I was.

Reflecting upon my past, I realize that the Lord never wanted me to live in misery and harm. He is not the author of confusion. Once I began to open the Bible and purposely look for answers to my problems, I found not only the answers, but a greater sense of purpose for my life. Only God can take misery and build a ministry.

I will strive to be a modern day Sarah. She was a wonderful, spirit-filled woman who dared to step out of her comfort zone and follow the One who leads invisibly. I, too, want to be remembered as a woman of God who was kept by her heavenly Father through His Son Jesus Christ and wrote the book *Testimony of a Kept Woman: From Misery to Ministry Instead of the State Penitentiary.*

And the Lord is with Jan...

PART FIVE:
reflections about domestic violence and emotional abuse

epilogue

You meant to hurt me, but God turned your evil into good.

Genesis 50:20 (ICB)

And we know that in everything God works for the good of those who love him. They are the people God called because that was his plan.

Romans 8:28 (ICB)

Praising God from a Position of Pain

In the last chapter of Genesis, Joseph's life ends with divine success. The Lord was with Joseph every step of his journey. His brothers' attempts to destroy him were unsuccessful because God had a divine purpose for Joseph's life. In the providence of God, all things worked together for good. The Lord has been with me, also. Let me tell you the rest of the story regarding my two former husbands.

Committing the Unthinkable

Vincent has typically continued to live reclusively in his same apartment that his family left him in over thirty years ago. His world has remained as unchanged, undisrupted, and predictable as the daily turning of the earth on its axis. However, four years ago, something happened that disturbed his daily routine and upset his life to the core. His ninety-eight year old mother became ill and asked Vincent to visit her. She wanted to discuss with him the details of her will and offer him the keys to the beautiful home she had willed to him. Believe it or not, he refused to visit her.

Although I had divorced her son many years earlier, my former mother-in-law and I continued to remain close, and we communicated frequently. We were more like a mother and daughter than in-laws. She confided in me how hurt she was that her own son still continued to remain distant and unloving after so many years. She then shared with me that she was dying, and she wanted her grandsons and me to attend her funeral. I promised her that we would be there for her. We both cried together over the phone, and I prayed with her. She passed away a few weeks later.

Dexter, Lawrence, and I flew to Philadelphia to attend her funeral. The family was overjoyed and welcomed the three of us with open arms. By the day of the funeral, everyone had arrived except Vincent. As the family members waited in the hall of the church, we all hoped against hope that he would have a change of heart and attend his mother's funeral. Even after we were all escorted into the sanctuary and the memorial service was about to begin, our eyes remained fixed on the church doors leading into the sanctuary. I believe we were all silently praying that Vincent would magically appear just in the nick of time. But to everyone's astonishment, Vincent never showed up. His vacant reserved space on the front row of the pews loomed larger than life and made his absence appear even more dreadful. This was the last straw!

It was utterly impossible for me to understand how anyone could be so selfish and cold-hearted. And it was at that moment that I mentally washed my hands of Vincent. I never intended to speak to him again.

Defiant, Yet Obedient

God, however, had different plans for me. A few days after returning home from the funeral, I was surprised when the Lord tenderly instructed me to call Vincent and witness to him about Jesus.

"What?" I said in an audible voice. "Lord, you must be joking! I can't talk to *that* man after what he did to his mother! I love you, Lord, but I can't do this!"

And as far as I was concerned, the matter was closed, shut, and sealed. After all, what God wanted me to do was unreasonable... wasn't it? Nobody calls up an ex-husband and witnesses to him about his lost soul after the two of you have been divorced for more than thirty-three years... and especially after he didn't even go to his own mother's funeral.

That's ludicrous! Right?

So, I said, "No way, Jose!" I felt justified in refusing to make the telephone call and went about my daily routine. This went on for several weeks; however, I was completely miserable. I began to feel tired and moody. I felt as though I were lugging around a load of heavy bricks on my back. Although I felt sick, I never once considered going to the doctor because I knew what my problem was. It was simple. I was out of the will of God. So after procrastinating for more than a month and becoming a total wreck in the process, I reluctantly gave in and called Vincent. As I dialed the phone, I prayed that he would be out. Naturally, no such luck. He was home (no great surprise there!), and he answered the phone on the second ring. After identifying myself and making small talk about the weather, I went completely speechless. I actually did not know what to say to him. I had not rehearsed my speech because, frankly, I didn't know how to talk to Vincent about Jesus. I had tried to witness to him many times during the almost twenty years we were married, but it never worked. So, in my way of thinking, "What in the world would make this time any different from all the other times?"

My speechlessness, however, was in the providence of God. The moment I stopped talking, Vincent went on the defensive and immediately began talking non-stop. He tried to explain to me why he had not attended his mother's funeral. He said his actions were justified and that he had made his peace with God.

God's Miraculous Turn of Events

I knew Vincent expected me to verbally attack him for his despicable behavior, and that was exactly what I wanted to do... But God turned the tables on us both, and instead of my telling Vincent what I thought of him, I spoke calm and soothing words. This was incredible. I didn't even recognize my own voice. And for the next two and a half hours, I witnessed over the phone to my former husband about the love and forgiveness of the Lord Jesus Christ. My words flowed easily and effortlessly. I didn't stammer or stutter one time. Occasionally, Vincent would ask me a question, and I not only knew the answer, but I was able to quote just the right Bible verse needed to make my point. It is strange and difficult to explain, but it was as if someone else were speaking instead of me.

Finally, after I had said everything the Lord had told me to say, I asked Vincent if he wanted to pray the prayer of salvation and ask Jesus to come into his life. I held my breath because I was prepared for him to refuse my invitation. But to my complete amazement, Vincent said, "Yes!" He wanted Jesus. Then he repeated the prayer after me and invited the Lord Jesus Christ to come into his life. At that moment, Vincent was saved. Over the telephone, he became a brand new man in Christ. I was so excited that I could have done a double cart wheel! After I explained to him what had happened to him spiritually, Vincent began to cry like a baby. Now I really was speechless. He told me that all of a sudden his anger and rage were gone, and he felt as light as a feather. He began to laugh and cry simultaneously. We both were so happy and excited. He then begged me to forgive him for all the wrong he had done to me. After I told him I had forgiven him a long time ago, he began to cry again.

The following day, I sent him a Bible, and he started to read it daily. I also committed to disciple my new convert once a month with Bible study and other biblical tools. Today, Vincent and I still meet for Bible study over the phone on the last Sunday of every month at four o'clock sharp in the evening Eastern Standard Time. I call him, and he then returns my call so that the phone bill is on him. Vincent is a transformed man who now witnesses to others about the love of Jesus Christ. He is no longer that mean and angry man who hates people. He has completely changed. He is beginning to build a relationship with his two sons and his two lovely granddaughters, Cheyenne and Blair. This is difficult, but they are all willing to try. His transformation has amazed all who see him in his community in Gary. He is often asked what has made this difference in his life. He always gives God the glory and credits the love of his Lord and Savior Jesus Christ.

Just like Joseph in the book of Genesis, this miracle was in the providence of God. Not only did God have a plan for my life, but God also had a plan for Vincent's life, and I was an integral part of the plan. God *does* work in mysterious ways.

A Sad Ending to a Great Beginning

Harry, on the other hand, is a different story altogether. After divorcing me and selling our lovely home, he married the younger woman from another state and relocated to Montgomery, Alabama. He and his new wife bought a beautiful new home and started their life together. He was called to pastor a church in his new location; however, the congregation was less accepting of him than his congregation in Texas had been. A few members considered him to be just an "outsider," and many of the others never fully embraced him as their pastor.

The honeymoon phase passed quickly in his marriage and in his ministry. He soon began experiencing serious problems in both areas of his life. After less than two years, his second marriage failed, and he was sued for divorce. Soon after that, the members of his second church became dissatisfied with their new pastor and voted him out. Generally, things have not gone well for him.

Wonders Never Cease

Harry recently called me to apologize for all the pain he had caused and asked me to marry him again. No, I did not laugh in his face (we were on the phone), nor did I gloat over "his chickens having come home to roost" (Galatians 6:7). I feel sorry for him, and I am praying that the Lord will once again use him mightily in the ministry because he is highly skilled and gifted.

The question is, "Can a leopard change his spots?" Probably not, but nothing is too hard for God. I constantly remind myself that "with God, all things are possible" (Matthew 19:26b). I never want to forget that "the steps of a good man are ordered by the Lord... though he fall, he shall not be utterly cast down: for the Lord upholdeth him with his hand" (Psalm 37:24).

Beginning Anew

On January 17, 2010, I answered my call to ministry and preached my initial sermon. On October 2, 2011, both Lawrence, my son, and I were ordained together by the "Old Eastern Missionary Baptist Association of NC" into the ministry of Jesus Christ. I am profoundly honored and blessed to have dual memberships with two pastors, two First Ladies, and two church families. At Sycamore Hill Missionary Church, my primary pastor is Dr. Howard W. Parker and my second pastor is Sidney A. Locks, Jr., of Cornerstone Missionary Baptist Church—both in Greenville, NC. Both pastors shared in the licensing and ordination ceremonies with me. I realize it is unusual to have two church memberships in the same city, but it works for me. Cornerstone has services from 8:45 to 10:30, and Sycamore Hill worships from 11:00 to 12:30. It's perfect.

I retired after teaching fifty years in public education. What a blessing! Now, my plans are to work full time in the ministry, write books, preach the gospel of Jesus Christ, and travel around the world sharing my testimony. Yes, I am truly a kept woman. The Lord Jesus Christ has kept me and taken me from being a victim of domestic violence and emotional abuse to becoming a victorious and vivacious survivor in Jesus Christ. Without Him, I never would have made it. Only a loving and all-wise God could have kept me and taken me from misery to ministry instead of spending the rest of my life in the state penitentiary or mental institution.

Planning to Marry Husband Number Three

Finally, I am thrilled to tell you that I plan to marry a third time. You can read all about my wedding plans in Revelation 19:7-9. It will be a marriage to end all others. And, as it is recorded in Revelation 21:2, Christ will redeem me (and His Church) as the symbol of the marriage of the Lamb. I, along with a great multitude in Heaven, will say with a loud voice, "Let us be glad and rejoice and give Him glory, for the marriage of the Lamb has come, and as His wife, I will have made myself ready." I will be arrayed in fine linen, clean and bright. I will be that bride adorned for the Bridegroom, the Lord Jesus Christ.

And with my perfect Husband, I will experience perfect love-agape love, for He gave Himself for me, even unto death, yea, the death of the cross. And, this time, I will gladly share my first and last love, Jesus Christ, with everyone. "And we know that all things are working together for good for those who love God" (Romans 8:28).

As the Lord has been with Joseph and Jan, may the Lord Jesus Christ be with you every step of the way. (Genesis 39-50).

PART SIX

group discussion
questions to ponder

1. Why do you feel some Christian women are attracted to physical or emotional abusers?

    _____

    _____

    _____

2. What are some reasons why a person chooses to remain in a violent or abusive relationship?

    _____

    _____

    _____

3. In your opinion, which is worse—physical abuse or emotional/psychological abuse? Explain your answer.

    _____

    _____

    _____

4. Are you critical of or sympathetic toward those involved in abusive and/or violent relationships? Explain.

    _____

    _____

    _____

5. List the early tell-tale signs of abuse of both husbands that should have warned Jan of impending danger.

    _____

    _____

    _____

6. Why do you think some Christians ignore symptoms or signs that are transparently clear to others?

    _____

    _____

    _____

7. What can be done to prevent young people from becoming victims of abuse or abusers themselves?

    _____

    _____

    _____

8. Explain what caused Jan to leave a physically violent marriage number one to re-enter a worse situation of emotional abuse in marriage number two?

    _____

    _____

    _____

9. What is the "key" that enabled Jan to overcome nearly half a century of victimization by domestic violence and emotional abuse and yet emerge victorious?

    _____

_____

_____

10. How can this vital "spiritual key" be taught to others?

_____

_____

_____

11. List the character traits that you admire least and/ or most about Jan. Explain your reasons.

_____

_____

_____

12. In your opinion, what personality traits caused Jan to become easily manipulated and victimized by both husbands?

_____

_____

_____

13. How can parents help protect their children from abusive relationships?

_____

_____

_____

14. In what ways did Jan's lack of self-esteem manifest itself in both marriages?

_____

_____

_____

15. What do you believe was the turning point in Jan's life that eventually brought her peace and fulfillment?

_____

_____

_____

16. What have you learned about God's love and care for you while reading *Testimony of a Kept Woman: From Misery to Ministry...Instead of the State Penitentiary?*

_____

_____

_____

_____

_____